ROYAL COURT

M000278875

The Royal Court Theatre presents

THE LOW ROAD
by **Bruce Norris**

THE LOW ROAD was first performed at The Royal Court Jerwood Theatre Downstairs, Sloane Square, on Friday 22nd March 2013.

THE LOW ROAD

by **Bruce Norris**

Cast in alphabetical order

Redcoat/Hessian/Questioner/Faraday/Musician **Jared Ashe**

Questioner/Musician **Jack Benjamin**

Sergeant Manley/Attendant/Musician **Kit Benjamin**

Mrs Trumpett/Belinda/Margarita Low **Elizabeth Berrington**

Peg/Sister Elizabeth/Musician **Helen Cripps**

Jim Trumpett **Johnny Flynn**

Company **Charlyne Francis**

Farmer/Nathaniel Pugh/Ed **Ian Gelder**

Hessian/Pandit **Raj Ghatak**

Old One-Eyed Tizzy/Ntombi/Mary Cleere **Natasha Gordon**

John Blanke **Kobna Holdbrook-Smith**

Prostitute/Constance Pugh/Questioner **Ellie Kendrick**

The Duke of Buccleuch/Hessian/Questioner/Officer **Edward Killingback**

Young Jim Trumpett **Frederick Neilson/Will Thompson**

Captain Shirley/Poor Tim/Dick Trumpett **Simon Paisley Day**

Adam Smith **Bill Paterson**

Slave Merchant/Brother Amos/Hessian/Ivan/Lagarde **Harry Peacock**

Prostitute/Sister Comfort/Delilah Low **Leigh Quinn**

Greasy-Haired Man/Martin/Isaac Low **John Ramm**

Company **Joseph Rowe**

All other parts played by members of the company

Director **Dominic Cooke**

Designer **Tom Pye**

Lighting Designer **Jean Kalman**

Sound Designer **Carolyn Downing**

Composer **Gary Yershon**

Casting Director **Amy Ball**

Associate Designer **Ben Gerlis**

Assistant Director **Simon Dormandy**

Production Manager **Tariq Rifaat**

Stage Manager **Nafeesah Butt**

Deputy Stage Manager **Sarah Hellicar**

Assistant Stage Managers **Katie Hutcheson & Sophie Rubenstein**

Stage Management Work Placements **Elena Rouse-Eyre & Amy Slater**

Costume Supervisors **Iona Kenrick & Jackie Orton**

Hair & Make-up Supervisor **Carole Hancock for HUM Studio**

Assistant Hair & Make-up Supervisor **Laura Solari**

Wigs supplied by **HUM Studio**

Dialect Coach **Penny Dyer**

Movement Directors **Imogen Knight & Sue Lefton**

Fight Director **Bret Yount**

Set Built by **Miraculous Engineering**

Scenic Work by **Kerry Jarrett**

Additional Scenic Elements by **Bay Productions & The Rocking Horse Workshop**

Armourer **Mark Shelley**

The Royal Court & Stage Management wish to thank the following for their help with this production: Jude Akuwudike, MAC Makeup, Peter Thompson, Dr Nick Phillipson, Dr Tim Lockley, Tim Stanley, Marie Lane, Sharon Foley, John Evans, Jan Archibald at London Wigs, Tricycle, Almeida, ETT, Young Vic, Malcolm Hart.

THE COMPANY

BRUCE NORRIS (Writer)

FOR THE ROYAL COURT: Clybourne Park, The Pain & the Itch.

OTHER THEATRE INCLUDES: Domesticated (Lincoln Center); A Parallelogram (Steppenwolf Theatre, Chicago/Mark Taper Forum); Clybourne Park, The Pain & the Itch (Playwrights Horizons, Steppenwolf); The Unmentionables, We All Went Down to Amsterdam, Purple Heart, The Infidel (Steppenwolf).

AWARDS INCLUDE: Tony Award for Best Play, Laurence Olivier Award for Best New Play, Evening Standard Theatre Award for Best New Play, Pulitzer Prize for Drama (Clybourne Park); Steinberg Playwrights Award, Whiting Prize, Joseph Jefferson Award (Chicago).

JARED ASHE (Redcoat/Hessian/Questioner/Faraday/Musician)

THEATRE INCLUDES: Radio Times (Watermill/tour); Privates on Parade (West Yorkshire Playhouse /Birmingham Rep); Black Coffee (Chichester Festival); A Midsummer Night's Dream, The Mikado (Stephen Joseph/tour); Oh, What A Lovely War! (The Haymarket Basingstoke); The Resistible Rise Of Arturo Ui (Watford Palace); Pinocchio (Hull Truck); Hot Mikado, Pick Yourself Up, The Taming of the Shrew, Up 'n' Under, The Merchant Of Venice, The Young Ones (Queen's Theatre, Hornchurch); Robin Hood (New Wolsey, Ipswich).

TELEVISION INCLUDES: MI High.

FILM INCLUDES: Chemical Wedding.

JACK BENJAMIN (Questioner/Musician)

THEATRE INCLUDES: Tiger Tail, Treasure Island (Southampton Nuffield).

FILM INCLUDES: No Salt.

AWARDS INCLUDE: The Laurence Olivier Bursary.

KIT BENJAMIN (Sergeant Manley/Attendant/Musician)

THEATRE INCLUDES: Floyd Collins (Southwark Playhouse); The Sound of Music (international tour); Bitter Sweet, Chicago (Century); Wild Orchids (Chichester Festival); In the Prison Colony (Baron's Court); Jolson (Victoria Palace/Royal Alexandra Theatre, Toronto); Buddy: The Buddy Holly Story (Novello); Cats (New London); The Producers (Theatre Royal, Drury Lane); Imagine This (Theatre Royal, Plymouth); Singin' in the Rain (UK tour); Dick Barton, Femme Fatale, The Mystery of Edwin Drood (Warehouse, Croydon).

TELEVISION INCLUDES: Casualty, The House of Elliott, The Chronicles of Narnia.

FILM INCLUDES: Fourteen Years On.

ELIZABETH BERRINGTON (Mrs Trumpett/Belinda/Margarita Low)

FOR THE ROYAL COURT: The Nocky (Royal Court Young Writers Festival).

OTHER THEATRE INCLUDES: Absent Friends (Harold Pinter); Abigail's Party (Hampstead/New Ambassador's); Top Girls (Oxford Stage Company); The Shagaround (Nuffield/Ashcroft, Croydon); The Country Wife (Crucible, Sheffield); Together (Edinburgh Festival Fringe); Y a Otra Cosa Mariposa (BAC); The Last Waltz (Gateway, Chester); An Ideal Husband (Royal Exchange, Manchester); The Left-over Heart (Offstage); Rupert Street Lonely Hearts Club (ETT/Donmar/Criterion).

TELEVISION INCLUDES: Being Eileen, Stella, Stage Door Johnnies, New Tricks, Lapland, Doctor Who, The Crimson Petal & the White, Waterloo Road, Psychoville, Jo Brand's Little Cracker, Moving Wallpaper, A Touch of Frost, Apparitions, Poirot, May Contain Nuts, Annually Retentive, Drop Dead Gorgeous, Love Lies Bleeding, Rose & Maloney, Missing, The Rotters Club, Where the Heart is, Shane, Family Business, The Deal, Bodily Harm, Rescue Me, The Chambers, The Bill, Sam's Game, The Grimleys,

The Vice, Let Them Eat Cake, Nature Boy, Casualty, The Lakes, Silent Witness, My Wonderful Life, The Moonstone, Nurses, Between the Lines.

FILM INCLUDES: Hard Boiled Sweets, In Bruges, Fred Claus, Are You Ready for Love, I Could Never Be Your Woman, Scoop, Nanny McPhee, A Cock & Bull Story, Secrets & Lies, Naked, Vera Drake, Spivs, Quills, Little Vampires, Mad Cows, Eight & a Half Women, Eugene Onegin, An Urban Ghost Story.

RADIO INCLUDES: Normal & Nat, Splash, Weird Tales.

DOMINIC COOKE (Director)

FOR THE ROYAL COURT: In the Republic of Happiness, Ding Dong the Wicked, Choir Boy, In Basildon, Chicken Soup with Barley, Clybourne Park (& West End), Aunt Dan & Lemon, The Fever, Seven Jewish Children, Wig Out!, Now or Later, War & Peace/Fear & Misery, Rhinoceros, The Pain & the Itch, Other People, Fireface, Spinning into Butter, Redundant, Fucking Games, Plasticine, The People Are Friendly, This is a Chair, Identical Twins.

OTHER THEATRE INCLUDES: Comedy of Errors (National); Arabian Nights, Pericles, The Winter's Tale, The Crucible, Postcards from America, As You Like It, Macbeth, Cymbeline, The Malcontent (RSC); By the Bog of Cats... (Wyndham's); The Eccentricities of a Nightingale (Gate, Dublin); Arabian Nights (Young Vic/UK & World tours/New Victory Theatre, New York); The Weavers, Hunting Scenes from Lower Bavaria (Gate); The Bullet (Donmar); Afore Night Come, Entertaining Mr Sloane (Clwyd); The Importance of Being Earnest (Atlantic Theatre Festival, Canada); Caravan (National Theatre of Norway); My Mother Said I Never Should (Oxford Stage Company/Young Vic); Kiss of the Spider Woman (Bolton Octagon); Of Mice & Men (Nottingham Playhouse); Autogeddon (Assembly Rooms).

OPERA INCLUDES: The Magic Flute (WNO); I Capuleti e i Montecchi, La Bohème (Grange Park Opera).

AWARDS INCLUDE: Laurence Olivier Awards for Best Director & Best Revival (The Crucible); TMA/Equity Award for Best Show for Young People (Arabian Nights); Fringe First Award (Autogeddon).

Dominic was Associate Director of the Royal Court 1999-2002, Associate Director of RSC 2002-2006 & Assistant Director RSC 1992-1993.

Dominic is Artistic Director of the Royal Court.

HELEN CRIPPS (Peg/Sister Elizabeth/Musician)

THEATRE INCLUDES: Julius Caesar (Donmar); Earthquakes in London (National/Headlong tour); Hotel (The Invisible Dot/Edinburgh Festival Fringe).

AS WRITER/PERFORMER, THEATRE INCLUDES: Mrs Biscuit (Hen & Chickens); Alex & Helen's Radio Nowhere (Just the Tonic); Happy Now? (Free Fringe); Wham Bam, Niceties (Cambridge Footlights).

TELEVISION INCLUDES: Anna & Katy, Teaboys, Horne & Corden.

FILM INCLUDES: Black Pond.

SIMON DORMANDY (Assistant Director)

AS DIRECTOR, THEATRE INCLUDES: Spring Awakening (Underbelly/Arcola); Summerfolk (Cochrane); The Mill on the Floss (Drama Studio); A Passage to India, Henry VI Pts I, II & III, The Rivals, Three Sisters, Waiting for Godot, The Kitchen, Journey's End, The Spanish Tragedy, The Suicide, The Relapse, King Lear, A Streetcar Named Desire, Richard III, Henry IV Pts I & 2, Habeas Corpus, Pool No Water, Joseph K, Attempts on her Life (Eton College).

AS PERFORMER, THEATRE INCLUDES: Vanity Fair, Pericles, Andromache, A Midsummer Night's Dream (Cheek by Jowl); The Plantagenets, The Country Wife, King Lear, Richard III, Twelfth Night, Measure for Measure, The Park (RSC); A Chorus of Disapproval, Antony & Cleopatra, (Birmingham Rep); The Liar (Old Vic); The Rivals (West Yorkshire Playhouse); Othello (Stephen Joseph, Scarborough); Death & the King's Horseman (Royal Exchange, Manchester); The Threepenny Opera (Donmar).

AS PERFORMER, TELEVISION/FILM INCLUDES: Vanity Fair, Little Dorrit.

CAROLYN DOWNING (Sound Designer)

FOR THE ROYAL COURT: Choir Boy, The Witness, Our Private Life, Oxford Street, Alaska.

OTHER THEATRE/OPERA INCLUDES: Fanny Och Alexander (Malmö Stadsteater); Love Song, Little Dogs (Frantic Assembly); Beautiful Burnout (Frantic Assembly/National Theatre of Scotland); Double Feature (National); King John, The Gods Weep, The Winter's Tale, Pericles, Days of Significance (RSC); Lower Ninth, Dimetos, Absurdia (Donmar); Angels in America, Millennium Approaches, Perestroika (Headlong); Amerika, Krieg der Bilder (Staatstheater Mainz); All My Sons (Broadway); Tre Kroner – Gustav III (Dramaten, Stockholm); Blackta, After Miss Julie, Ghosts, Dirty Butterfly (Young Vic); Lulu, The Kreutzer Sonata, Vanya, State of Emergency, The Internationalist (Gate, Notting Hill); After Dido (ENO); Gambling (Soho); Belongings (Hampstead); Andersen's English, Flight Path (Out Of Joint); To Kill A Mockingbird, The Country Wife, A Whistle In The Dark, Moonshed (Royal Exchange, Manchester); Blood Wedding (Almeida); The Water Engine (503/Young Vic); Stallerhof, No Way Out (Southwark); After Miss Julie, Othello (Salisbury); The Watery Part of the World (Sound & Fury); Gone To Earth (Shared Experience); If That's All There Is, Hysteria (Inspector Sands); 3rd Ring Out (Metis Arts).

CHARLYNE FRANCIS (Company)

THEATRE INCLUDES: The Unwanted (AG Productions); The Container (Chapter Arts); Breach (DSBC); Danny's Deal (Old Vic New Voices); Platform (Old Vic Tunnels); Handa's Hen (Little Angel); Nobody Lives Forever (Y Touring); Dirty Wonderland (Frantic Assembly); Don't Look Back (Dreamthinkspeak).

TELEVISION INCLUDES: Jack Whitehall's Secret Census.

FILM INCLUDES: If Only…

JOHNNY FLYNN (Jim Trumpett)

FOR THE ROYAL COURT: Jerusalem (West End), The Heretic.

OTHER THEATRE INCLUDES: Richard III, Twelfth Night (Globe/Apollo); The Taming of the Shrew, Twelfth Night (Propeller: Old Vic/international tour).

TELEVISION INCLUDES: Kingdom, Holby City, Murder in Suburbia.

FILM INCLUDES: Something in the Air, Lotus Eaters, Crusade in Jeans.

RADIO INCLUDES: Romeo & Juliet.

IAN GELDER (Farmer/Nathaniel Pugh/Ed)

FOR THE ROYAL COURT: Fire Face, Mouth to Mouth (Albery).

OTHER THEATRE INCLUDES: King Lear (Almeida); Definitely the Bahamas (Orange Tree); Company, Racing Demon (Crucible, Sheffield); Precious Little Talent (Trafalgar Studios); Lingua Franca (Finborough /59E59); The Power of Yes, Henry IV Parts I & II, His Dark Materials, Stuff Happens (National); The Sound of Music (Palladium); The Crucible (& Gielgud), The Taming of the Shrew (& Queen's/Kennedy Center), Titus Andronicus, The Merchant of Venice (& international tour), Richard III, Privates on Parade (& Piccadilly), Henry VI, As You Like It (RSC); Serious Money, Divine Right (Birmingham Rep); A Passage to India, Anna Karenina, Heartbreak House (Shared Experience); Three Sisters (Chichester Festival); Richard II, Pal Joey (Bristol Old Vic); Martin Yesterday (Royal Exchange, Manchester); Front Page, Good (Donmar); Marvin's Room (Comedy); Mrs Warren's Profession (Lyric, Hammersmith); Poor Super Man (& Traverse), Apocalyptica (Hampstead).

TELEVISION INCLUDES: Game of Thrones, Mr Selfridge, Endeavour, Psychoville, Torchwood, Silent Witness, Robin Hood, Fallen Angel, The Commander, Poirot, The Day Today, Absolutely Fabulous, Kavanagh QC, Blackeyes.

FILM INCLUDES: Pope Joan, The Emissary, Jinnah, King Ralph, Little Dorritt, The Fool.

RAJ GHATAK (Hessian/Pandit)

FOR THE ROYAL COURT: The Spiral, Shades (Unheard Voices), Free Outgoing.

OTHER THEATRE INCLUDES: Golgotha (Tristan Bates); Soho Cinders, A Journey Remembered (Soho); The Secret Garden (Edinburgh Festival/Royal Alexandria, Toronto); The Absent Lover (international tour); The Great Extension, High Heel Parrotfish, Airport 2000 (Theatre Royal Stratford East); Simply Cinderella (Curve); Tales from Firozsha Baag (National Theatre Studio); Bombay Dreams (Apollo Victoria); Hijra (Bush/West Yorkshire Playhouse); My Dad's Corner Shop (Birmingham Rep); West Side Story (Prince of Wales); Bollywood or Bust (Watermans Theatre/tour); East is East (Oldham Coliseum); Don't Look at my Sister Innit! (Bloomsbury Theatre/Watermans); Arrange That Marriage (Bloomsbury); Nagwanti (Tara Arts).

TELEVISION INCLUDES: Doctors, Dead Set, Sinchronicity, All About Me, Hard Cash, Out of Sight.

FILM INCLUDES: Naachle London, Diary of a Thagee, Karma Magnet, Dangerous Parking, Starter for 10, The Lives of the Saints, Never Say Never Mind, Birthday Girl, Sari & Trainers.

NATASHA GORDON (Old One-Eyed Tizzy/Ntombi/Mary Cleere)

FOR THE ROYAL COURT: Clubland.

OTHER THEATRE INCLUDES: Red Velvet (Tricycle); Speechless (Shared Experience/Sherman Cymru); Mules, Arabian Nights (& West End), The Exception & the Rule (Young Vic); As You Like It, The Tamer Tamed, Cymbeline (RSC); Inside Out (Arcola/tour); Skin Deep (Warehouse, Croydon); Aladdin (Lyric, Hammersmith); Top Girls (BAC).

TELEVISION INCLUDES: Secrets & Worlds, Open Doors – A Study in Time, Law & Order UK, 10 Days to War, Doctors, EastEnders, Little Miss Jocelyn, Holby City, The Bill.

KOBNA HOLDBROOK-SMITH (John Blanke)

FOR THE ROYAL COURT: Feast (with Young Vic).

OTHER THEATRE INCLUDES: Antigone, Death & the King's Horseman (National); The Changeling, Joe Turner's Come & Gone, The Water Engine (& 503), A Respectable Wedding (Young Vic); Light Shining in Buckinghamshire (Arcola); Detaining Justice, Seize the Day, Category B, Fabulation, Gem of the Ocean, Walk Hard – Talk Loud, The Playboy of the West Indies (Tricycle); 50 Ways to Leave Your Lover (Bush); Love's Labour's Lost, We, the People (Globe); Ma Rainey's Black Bottom (Royal Exchange, Manchester); Mother Courage & Her Children, 3 Tales of Courage (Eclipse).

TELEVISION INCLUDES: Frankie, The Café, Silk, Sirens, Whites, Phone Shop, The Persuasionists, Katy Brand's Big Ass Show, Sorry I've Got No Head, Little Britain, Harry & Paul, Pulling, Taking the Flak, Star Stories, Whatever it Takes, Whistleblowers, Saxondale, Cul de Sac, Mike Bassett, According to Bex, Absolute Power, Cyderdelic, Semi-Detached, The Bunker, Judge John Deed.

FILM INCLUDES: The Double, Roadkill, 10ml, Womack, Rahab, Timed.

RADIO INCLUDES: Direct Red, Final Demands, Moby Dick, The Patience of Mr Job, The Black Bono, Abi Hour, Bigipedia, Dr No.

JEAN KALMAN (Lighting Designer)

FOR THE ROYAL COURT: Motortown, Lucky Dog, The Fever, Blasted.

OTHER THEATRE INCLUDES: School for Scandal (Barbican); Macbeth (RSC); Festen (Almeida/West End); Cabaret, The Beautiful Game, By the Bog Of Cats…(West End); John Gabriel Borkman (Abbey/Brooklyn Academy of Music); In the Red & Brown Water (Young Vic); The Year of Magical Thinking (National/ tour); Mother Courage, Peter Brook's The Cherry Orchard, White Chameleon, The Mahabharata, Richard III, Woza Albert, The Tempest, Macbeth, King Lear, Richard III, A Midsummer Night's Dream, The PowerBook, Happy Days (National); The Crucible, Romeo & Juliet, Julius Caesar, Little Eyolf, Pericles (RSC); The Book Of Grace (Public, NYC).

OPERA CREDITS INCLUDE: Médée (Theatre Champs Elysee); The Marriage of Figaro, Messiah (& Lyon), La Bohème, Così fan tutte, Death in Venice (& Brussels/La Scala), Peter Grimes, Lohengrin, Der Rosenkavalier, Mary Stuart, Semele (ENO); Dionysus (Salzburger Festspiele, De Nederlandse Opera, Staatsoper Im Schiller Theatre); Don Giovanni (Opera Lyon/Grand Theatre de Geneve); Attila, Macbeth (The Met Opera, NYC); Alcina (La Scala/Vienna State Opera); La Traviata, The Turn of the Screw, Giulio Cesare (Royal Opera House); Boris Gudonuv (Teatro La Fenice); Guillaume Tell, Die Zauberflote, Parsifal, Castor et Pollux, St Francois D'Asisse, Marco Polo, La Juive (Netherlands Opera); Dialogues Des Carmelites (Opera de Oviedo/Vlaamse Opera/Opera de Nice); Eugene Onegin (Lyric Opera of Chicago/The Met Opera, NYC/ENO); Pelleas et Melisande, Death In Venice, Iphigenie en Aulide/Iphigenie en Tauride (La Monnaie, Brussels); Dido & Aeneas, Carmen (Opera Comique/international tour); Così fan tutte (Festival D'Aix En Provence); La Damnation De Faust, Romeo & Juliet (Napoli Teatro); La Bohème (Deutsche Opera am Rhein); Così fan tutte/Les Noces De Figaro (Lyon Opera).

AWARDS INCLUDE: Laurence Olivier Award for Best Lighting Design (Richard III/White Chameleon); Evening Standard Theatre Award for Best Lighting (Festen).

ELLIE KENDRICK (Prostitute/Constance Pugh/Questioner)

FOR THE ROYAL COURT: In the Republic of Happiness.

OTHER THEATRE INCLUDES: Romeo & Juliet (Globe).

TELEVISION INCLUDES: Game of Thrones, Being Human, Upstairs Downstairs, The Diary of Anne Frank, Lewis, Prime Suspect, Doctors, In2Minds, Waking the Dead.

FILM INCLUDES: Cheerful Weather for the Wedding, An Education.

RADIO INCLUDES: Dracula, Life & Fate, Plantagenet, Words & Music, The Resistance of Mrs Brown, The Shooting Party, Lady from the Sea.

EDWARD KILLINGBACK (The Duke of Buccleuch/Hessian/Questioner/Officer)

FOR THE ROYAL COURT: Posh (West End).

OTHER THEATRE INCLUDES: Seven (Invertigo/George Tavern).

FREDERICK NEILSON (Young Jim Trumpett)

THEATRE INCLUDES: A Christmas Carol (Talkwood/tour)

Frederick attends drama classes at NLPAC.

SIMON PAISLEY DAY (Captain Shirley/Poor Tim/Dick Trumpett)

FOR THE ROYAL COURT: The Ugly One.

OTHER THEATRE INCLUDES: The Taming of the Shrew, Timon of Athens (Globe); Private Lives (Theatre Royal, Bath/West End/Broadway); Twelfth Night, Love's Labour's Lost, Anything Goes, The Coast of Utopia, Hamlet, Albert Speer, Candide, Money, Troilus & Cressida, Oh! What a Lovely War (National); Entertaining Mr Sloane (Trafalgar Studios); Don't Look Now (Lyric, Hammersmith); The 39 Steps (Criterion); The Philanthropist (Donmar); Cymbeline, Twelfth Night (Regent's Park); Anything Goes (Theatre Royal, Drury Lane); Measure for Measure (AFTLS); By Jeeves! (Duke of York's); A Woman of No Importance (RSC/Theatre Royal Haymarket); seasons at Harrogate; Stephen Jospeh, Scarborough; Citizens'; Bristol Old Vic; Crucible, Sheffield & the Orange Tree.

TELEVISION INCLUDES: Family Tree, Big Bad World, Da Vinci's Demons, Titanic, Sherlock, Doc Martin, Hustle, Being Human, Midsomer Murders, The Relief of Belsen, Mr Loveday's Little Outing, Space Race, Doctor Who, He Knew He was Right, Spartacus, Bertie & Elizabeth, House of Elliott, Red Dwarf, The Great Kandinsky, Pie in the Sky.

FILM INCLUDES: The Eagle of the Ninth, Flawless, The Queen of Sheba's Pearls, Churchill: The Hollywood Years, The Heart of Me, The Anorak, Diary, The Painting.

AWARDS INCLUDE: The Wandering Jew, Under the Net, Change of Heart.

BILL PATERSON (Adam Smith)

FOR THE ROYAL COURT: Death & the Maiden, A Man with Connections, And Me wi' a Bad Leg Tae.

OTHER THEATRE INCLUDES: And No More Shall We Part (Hampstead/Traverse); Earthquakes in London (National/Headlong); The Marriage Play, Good Person of Szechwan, Schweyk in the Second World War, Guys & Dolls (National); Ivanov (Almeida); Misery (Criterion); Crime & Punishment (Lyric, Hammersmith); Whose Life is it Anyway? (Savoy); Ella (ICA); Writer's Cramp (Hampstead/Bush); Treetops (Riverside); A Mongrel's Heart, Willie Rough (Lyceum); Little Red Hen, The Cheviot, The Stag & the Black Black Oil, The Game's a Bogey (7:84); Great Northern Welly Boot Show (Edinburgh Festival Fringe).

TELEVISION INCLUDES: The Man Who Crossed Hitler, Doctor Who, Miss Marple, The Forgotten Fallen, Law & Order UK, Into the Storm, Little Dorrit, Criminal Justice, Sea of Souls, Foyle's War, Danielle Cable: Eye Witness, Dr Zhivago, Othello, Rebel Heart, Wives & Daughters, Mr White Goes to Westminster, Melissa, The Writing on the Wall, The Crow Road, The Turnaround, Oliver's Travels, Hard Times, Wall of Silence, Tell Tale Hearts, Murder Most Horrid, Shrinks, Traffik, God on the Rocks, Yellowbacks, The Interrogation of John, The Singing Detective, Auf Wiedersehen Pet, Lily My Love, Dutch Girls, One of Ourselves, Stan's Last Game, Smiley's People, The Cherry Orchard, United Kingdom, The Lost Tribe, The Vanishing Army, Telford's Change, Licking Hitler, The Cheviot, The Stag & the Black Black Oil.

FILM INCLUDES: The White Room, Creation, How to Lose Friends & Alienate People, Miss Potter, Amazing Grace, Kingdom of Heaven, Bright Young Things, Sunshine, Hilary & Jackie, Spice World, Richard III, Victory, Truly Madly Deeply, Chaplin, The Adventures of Baron Munchausen, Return of the Musketeers, The Witches, Friendship's Death, Defence of the Realm, A Private Function, Comfort & Joy, The Killing Fields, The Ploughman's Lunch, The Odd Job.

RADIO INCLUDES: The Hitch-Hikers Guide to the Galaxy, Tinker Tailor Soldier Spy, and his own radio stories, Tales from the Back Green.

AWARDS INCLUDE: BAFTA (Scotland) Award for Best Actor (The Crow Road); The Stage Edinburgh Fringe Award 2012 for Best Actor (And No More Shall We Part).

HARRY PEACOCK (Slave Merchant/Brother Amos/Hessian/Ivan/Lagarde)

FOR THE ROYAL COURT: Chicken Soup with Barley.

OTHER THEATRE INCLUDES: Ladykillers (Fiery Angel); The Cherry Orchard (Birmingham Rep); As You Like It (Crucible, Sheffield/RSC); The Dark River (Orange Tree); Cinderella (Oxford Playhouse); Damned by Despair (Gate); Macbeth, Henry IV Parts I & II, His Dark Materials, Cyrano de Bergerac (National); The Recruiting Offficer (Litchfield); Oh! What a Lovely War, As You Like It, Romeo & Juliet (Regent's Park); The School for Scandal (Derby/Northampton).

TELEVISION INCLUDES: Bad Education, Starlings, Grandma's House, Toast, Walk on the Wild Side, Doctor Who, Midsomer Murders, Pie in the Sky, Wire in the Blood, The Bill, Star Stories, Kingdom, Keen Eddie, Jonathan Creek, Band of Brothers.

FILM INCLUDES: Gulliver's Travels, Judas, Valiant, Station Jim, High Adventure, The Banker, I Just Want to Kiss You.

TOM PYE (Designer)

FOR THE ROYAL COURT: NSFW, Fewer Emergencies.

OTHER THEATRE INCLUDES: Mother Courage, Major Barbara (National); John Gabriel Borkman (Abbey); All My Sons, Top Girls, Cyrano de Bergerac, Fiddler on the Roof, The Glass Menagerie (Broadway); Julius Caesar (Barbican/tour); The PowerBook, Medea (West End/Broadway); Sinatra (West End); Measure for Measure (Complicité/world tour).

DANCE INCLUDES: Shoes (Sadler's Wells).

OPERA INCLUDES: Cunning Little Vixen (Glyndebourne); Misfortune (Bregenz Festival/Royal Opera House); The Death of Klinghoffer, Eugene Onegin (ENO with MET); Elegy For Young Lovers, Messiah, Riders to the Sea, Orfeo, Death in Venice (ENO/La Scala, Milan); Così fan tutte, Les Noces de Figaro, Don Giovanni (Lyon); The Rape of Lucretia (Bayerischen Staatsoper, Munich).

LEIGH QUINN (Prostitute/Sister Comfort/Delilah Low)

THEATRE INCLUDES: Dancing at Lughnasa, What the Dickens! (Tobacco Factory); Time & the Conways (Circomedia, Bristol); Tom Jones (tour).

TELEVISION INCLUDES: Case Histories, Best of Men, Stakeout, Hedz.

FILM INCLUDES: Mad Bear & the Office Girl, 8 Minutes Idle, TATE Movie Project.

RADIO INCLUDES: All the Milkman's Children, The Fred McAulay Show.

JOHN RAMM (Greasy-Haired Man/Martin/Isaac Low)

THEATRE INCLUDES: The Merry Wives of Windsor, Pedro the Great Pretender, Dog in a Manger, Hamlet, Epicoene, Have, The Fool (RSC); The Physicists, Good (Donmar); 66 Books, Little Dolls, Flooded Grave (Bush); Much Ado About Nothing (Wyndham's); The Deep Blue Sea (West Yorkshire Playhouse); The Cherry Orchard, The Swineherd Prince, Uncle Vanya (Birmingham Rep); The Goat, or, Who is Sylvia? (Traverse); Breakfast at Tiffany's (Theatre Royal Haymarket); A Christmas Carol (Rose, Kingston); Tartuffe (Liverpool Playhouse); Ring Round the Moon (Playhouse); Nicholas Nickleby, King Lear (Chichester Festival); And Then There Were None (Gielgud); Twelfth Night (Royal Exchange, Manchester); The Green Man (Drum, Plymouth/Bush); The Golden Ass, A Midsummer Night's Dream, Cymbeline (Globe); Buried Alive (Drum, Plymouth/Hampstead); Rough Crossing (Watford Palace); The Winter's Tale (Salisbury Playhouse); Measure for Measure (Barbican); An Inspector Calls (Garrick); Time & the Room (& Edinburgh Festival Fringe), The Nose (Nottingham Playhouse); The Cabinet of Dr. Caligari (Lyric, Hammersmith); Rhinoceros (Man in the Moon); Great Expectations (Oxford Stage Company); The Messiah, Love upon the Throne, The Wonders of Sex, Shakespeare: The Truth! (National Theatre of Brent).

OPERA INCLUDES: Cherubin (Royal Opera House); The Threepenny Opera (Scottish Opera).

TELEVISION INCLUDES: Count Arthur Strong, Kevin Eldon Pilot, Twenty Twelve, Midsomer Murders, Doctors, Krod Mandoon, My Family, Foyle's War, The Palace, Losing It, Being Dom Joly, The Queen's Nose, Massive Landmarks of the 20th Century, People Like Us, The Bill, South of the Border.

FILM INCLUDES: Love Punch, Food of Love, The Nine Lives of Thomas Katz, Shakespeare in Love.

RADIO INCLUDES: Rumpole & the Explosive Evidence, A Nursery Tale, Inspector Steine, The Patrick & Maureen Maybe Music Experience, Broadcasting House, Private Passions, The Complete & Utter History of the Mona Lisa, Daughter of the Air, The Arts & How They Was Done, Iconic Icons.

JOSEPH ROWE (Company)

THEATRE INCLUDES: Pieces of Vincent (Arcola); Macbeth (Broadway); The Fear (Birmingham Library); Of Mice & Men (Black Box).

TELEVISION INCLUDES: Persona.

FILM INCLUDES: The Tower, The Lodger.

WILL THOMPSON (Young Jim Trumpett)

Will is making his professional stage debut in THE LOW ROAD.

Will is currently training at the Italia Conti Academy of Arts.

GARY YERSHON (Composer)

FOR THE ROYAL COURT: Chicken Soup with Barley, Rhinoceros, Redundant, Plasticine, Fireface.

OTHER THEATRE INCLUDES: Arabian Nights, Noughts & Crosses, Pericles, The Winter's Tale (2002 & 2006), The Crucible, As You Like It (1992 & 2005), Cymbeline, Macbeth, The Malcontent, Twelfth Night, The Taming of the Shrew, The Rivals, Hamlet, Don Carlos, The Devil is an Ass, Artists & Admirers, The Virtuoso (RSC); The Comedy of Errors, Grief, 2000 Years, Buried Child, The Duchess of Malfi, The Way of the World, Volpone, The Tempest, Broken Glass, Pericles, Troilus & Cressida, Widowers' Houses, Further than the Furthest Thing, Life X 3 (National); Julius Caesar, Boston Marriage, The Threepenny Opera (Donmar); Art, The Unexpected Man, The God of Carnage, The Play What I Wrote (West End/Broadway); The Norman Conquests (Old Vic/Broadway); Deathtrap (West End), plus scores for the Almeida; Young Vic; Gate, Notting Hill; Arcola; Regent's Park; Shared Experience; West Yorkshire Playhouse; Chichester Festival; Unicorn; Royal Exchange, Manchester; Manchester Library; Bristol Old Vic; Theatr Clwyd; Oxford Stage Company; Derby Playhouse; Nottingham Playhouse; Cheltenham Everyman; York Theatre Royal & Duke's Playhouse Lancaster.

TELEVISION INCLUDES: Trial & Retribution, Ebb & Flo, James the Cat, Painted Tales, The Heritage Game, Skin Deep.

FILM INCLUDES: Topsy-Turvy, Happy-Go-Lucky, Another Year, A Running Jump, Swim.

RADIO INCLUDES: Gawain & the Green Knight, Autumn Journal, Troilus & Criseyde, The Theban Plays, The Yellow Wallpaper, The Eve of St Agnes, The Odyssey, The Emigrants, Ruslan & Ludmila, The Wasting Game.

THE ENGLISH STAGE COMPANY
AT THE ROYAL COURT THEATRE

'For me the theatre is really a religion or way of life. You must decide what you feel the world is about and what you want to say about it, so that everything in the theatre you work in is saying the same thing ... A theatre must have a recognisable attitude. It will have one, whether you like it or not.'

George Devine, first artistic director of the English Stage Company: notes for an unwritten book.

photo: Stephen Cummiskey

As Britain's leading national company dedicated to new work, the Royal Court Theatre produces new plays of the highest quality, working with writers from all backgrounds, and addressing the problems and possibilities of our time.

"The Royal Court has been at the centre of British cultural life for the past 50 years, an engine room for new writing and constantly transforming the theatrical culture." Stephen Daldry

Since its foundation in 1956, the Royal Court has presented premieres by almost every leading contemporary British playwright, from John Osborne's Look Back in Anger to Caryl Churchill's A Number and Tom Stoppard's Rock 'n' Roll. Just some of the other writers to have chosen the Royal Court to premiere their work include Edward Albee, John Arden, Richard Bean, Samuel Beckett, Edward Bond, Leo Butler, Jez Butterworth, Martin Crimp, Ariel Dorfman, Stella Feehily, Christopher Hampton, David Hare, Eugène Ionesco, Ann Jellicoe, Terry Johnson, Sarah Kane, David Mamet, Martin McDonagh, Conor McPherson, Joe Penhall, Lucy Prebble, Mark Ravenhill, Simon Stephens, Wole Soyinka, Polly Stenham, David Storey, Debbie Tucker Green, Arnold Wesker and Roy Williams.

"It is risky to miss a production there." Financial Times

In addition to its full-scale productions, the Royal Court also facilitates international work at a grass roots level, developing exchanges which bring young writers to Britain and sending British writers, actors and directors to work with artists around the world. The research and play development arm of the Royal Court Theatre, The Studio, finds the most exciting and diverse range of new voices in the UK. The Studio runs play-writing groups including the Young Writers Programme, Critical Mass for black, Asian and minority ethnic writers and the biennial Young Writers Festival. For further information, go to www.royalcourttheatre.com/playwriting/the-studio.

"Yes, the Royal Court is on a roll. Yes, Dominic Cooke has just the genius and kick that this venue needs... It's fist-bitingly exciting." Independent

Spring 2013

ROYAL COURT

Jerwood Theatre Upstairs

5 Apr–4 May 2013

a new play
by Anthony Neilson

Neilson is renowned for his ground-breaking
and imaginative new work.

11 May–8 Jun 2013
A Royal Court Theatre and Fuel co-production

the victorian in the wall
by Will Adamsdale

Perrier Award winner Adamsdale's new play contains jokes, songs,
banging on recycling boxes, a talking fridge......

020 7565 5000
www.royalcourttheatre.com

⊖ Sloane Square ⇌ Victoria ▣ royalcourt ◼ theroyalcourttheatre

Principal Sponsor **Coutts**

Supported using public funding by
**ARTS COUNCIL
ENGLAND**

**ROYAL COURT
BAR & KITCHEN**

Our Bar and Kitchen serves an array of
seasonal food from quick snacks to pre-
show dining. Carefully selected wines, a
wide range of teas, coffees and aperitivos
are offered throughout the day.

Opening Hours
Monday – Friday: 11am – late, Saturday: 12pm – late
Lunch served 12 – 3pm, Dinner served 5 – 8pm

To make a reservation call **020 7565 5058** or or book online
www.royalcourttheatre.com/bar

ROYAL COURT SUPPORTERS

The Royal Court has significant and longstanding relationships with many organisations and individuals who provide vital support. It is this support that makes possible its unique playwriting and audience development programmes.

Coutts is the Principal Sponsor of the Royal Court. The Genesis Foundation supports the Royal Court's work with International Playwrights. Theatre Local is sponsored by Bloomberg. The Jerwood Charitable Foundation supports new plays by playwrights through the Jerwood New Playwrights series. The Andrew Lloyd Webber Foundation supports the Royal Court's Studio, which aims to seek out, nurture and support emerging playwrights.

The Harold Pinter Playwright's Award is given annually by his widow, Lady Antonia Fraser, to support a new commission at the Royal Court.

Principal Sponsor

Supported by
ARTS COUNCIL ENGLAND

INDIVIDUAL MEMBERS

THE LOW ROAD PRODUCTION PARTNERS

Eric Abraham

MAJOR DONORS

Anonymous
Rob and Siri Cope
Cas Donald
Jack & Linda Keenan
Adam Kenwright
Miles Morland
NoraLee & Jon Sedmak
Jan & Michael Topham
Stuart & Hilary Williams
Charitable Foundation

MOVER-SHAKERS

Eric Abraham
Anonymous
Christine Collins
Piers & Melanie Gibson
Lydia & Manfred Gorvy
Mr & Mrs Roderick Jack
Duncan Matthews QC
Ian & Carol Sellars
Nicholas Stanley
Edgar & Judith Wallner

BOUNDARY-BREAKERS

Anonymous
Katie Bradford
David Harding
Steve Kingshott
Philip & Joan Kingsley
Emma Marsh
Philippa Thorp
Mr & Mrs Nick Wheeler

GROUND-BREAKERS

Anonymous
Allen Appen & Jane Wiest
Moira Andreae
Mr & Mrs Simon Andrews
Nick Archdale
Charlotte Asprey
Jane Attias
Brian Balfour-Oatts
Elizabeth & Adam Bandeen
Ray Barrell & Ursula Van Almsick
Dr Kate Best
Sarah & David Blomfield

Stan & Val Bond
Kristina Borsy & Nick Turdean
Neil & Sarah Brener
Deborah Brett
Joanna Buckenham
Lois Moore & Nigel Burridge
Louise Burton
Helena Butler
Sindy & Jonathan Caplan
Gavin & Lesley Casey
Sarah & Philippe Chappatte
Tim & Caroline Clark
Carole & Neville Conrad
Andrea & Anthony Coombs
Clyde Cooper
Ian & Caroline Cormack
Mr & Mrs Cross
Andrew & Amanda Cryer
Alison Davies
Roger & Alison De Haan
Noel De Keyzer
Matthew Dean
Polly Devlin OBE
Sophie Diedrichs-Cox
Denise & Randolph Dumas
Robyn Durie
Zeina Durra & Saadi Soudavar
Glenn & Phyllida Earle
The Edwin Fox Foundation
Lisa Erikson & Edward Ocampo
Mark & Sarah Evans
Margaret Exley CBE
Celeste & Peter Fenichel
Deborah Ferreira
Beverley Gee
Nick & Julie Gould
Lord & Lady Grabiner
Richard & Marcia Grand
Reade & Elizabeth Griffith
Sue & Don Guiney
Jill Hackel & Andrzej Zarzycki
Carol Hall
Jennifer & Stephen Harper
Sam & Caroline Haubold
Madeleine Hodgkin

Mr & Mrs Gordon Holmes
Damien Hyland
Suzie & David Hyman
Amanda Ibbetson
Nicholas Jones
David P Kaskel & Christopher A Teano
Vincent & Amanda Keaveny
Peter & Maria Kellner
Nicola Kerr
Mr & Mrs Pawel Kisielewski
David & Sarah Kowitz
Rosemary Leith
Larry & Peggy Levy
Imelda Liddiard
Daisy & Richard Littler
Kathryn Ludlow
Beatrice & James Lupton CBE
Dr Ekaterina Malievskaia & George Goldsmith
Christopher Marek Rencki
Andrew McIver
Barbara Minto
Angelie Moledina
Ann & Gavin Neath CBE
Clive & Annie Norton
Georgia Oetker
James Orme-Smith
Mr & Mrs Sandy Orr
Mr & Mrs Guy Paterson
Sir William & Lady Vanessa Patey
William Plapinger & Cassie Murray
Andrea & Hilary Ponti
Lauren Prakke
Annie & Preben Prebensen
Mrs Ivetta Rabinovich
Julie Ritter
Mark & Tricia Robinson
Paul & Gill Robinson
Corinne Rooney
Sir & Lady Ruddock
William & Hilary Russell
Julie & Bill Ryan
Sally & Anthony Salz
Bhags Sharma
J Sheridan
The Michael & Melanie Sherwood Charitable Foundation

Tom Siebens & Mimi Parsons
Andy Simpkin
Anthony Simpson & Susan Boster
Andrea Sinclair & Serge Kremer
Paul & Rita Skinner
Mr & Mrs RAH Smart
Brian Smith
Barbara Soper
Sue St Johns
The Ulrich Family
The Ury Trust
Amanda Vail
Constanze Von Unruh
Ian & Victoria Watson & The Watson Foundation
Matthew & Sian Westerman
Anne-Marie Williams
Sir Robert & Lady Wilson
Mr Daniel Winterfeldt & Mr Jonathan Leonhart
Martin & Sally Woodcock
Katherine & Michael Yates

With thanks to our Friends, Stage-Taker and Ice-Breaker members whose support we greatly appreciate.

APPLAUDING
THE EXCEPTIONAL.

Coutts is proud to sponsor the Royal Court Theatre

THE LOW ROAD

Bruce Norris

Characters

ACT TWO

BELINDA
ED
DICK
PANDIT
NTOMBI
MARTIN
IVAN
MALE 1 (*voice*)
MALE 2 (*voice*)
ATTENDANT
MALE 3 (*voice*)
FEMALE
ISAAC LOW
MARGARITA LOW
FOOTMAN
DELILAH LOW
SERVANT (FARADAY)
LAGARDE
MARY CLEERE
OFFICERS 1, 2 *and* 3
ALIENS 1 *and* 2

Also PROTESTERS, SECURITY POLICE, SERVANTS,
ACTORS, DINNER GUESTS, SOLDIERS.

Note on the Text

Dialogue spoken simultaneously is laid out in columns; where
many characters are speaking simultaneously, a thin vertical line
also runs alongside the text.

German translations by Barbara Christ.

*This text went to press before the end of rehearsals and so may
differ slightly from the play as performed.*

Author's Note

The set should be open and flexible and suggest the plain,
whitewashed interior of a New England meeting house *circa*
1790. Several doors open onto the stage. All other scenery –
stairs, tables, etc. – should be introduced into this space as
necessary to establish a scene. When Act Two begins, the visual
change should conceal the look of Act One. Then, of course, we
return to the original configuration for the remainder of the act.

The time is from 1759–1776, with a brief detour to the present.

As to accents – since no one really knows what anyone sounded
like in the late 1700s, I'd suggest that some distinction be made
between the English characters (such as Shirley) and the
thoroughly American ones. And if Jim's accent is
anachronistically American-contemporary, all the better.

B.N.

ACT ONE

*Before house lights darken, a door at the back of the stage opens
and* ADAM SMITH – that *Adam Smith* – *enters, walking stick in
hand, dressed in a greatcoat and tricorne hat. He carefully
removes these, hanging them on pegs by the door, then shuffles
toward a small lectern, clutching a leather folio. A nearby sign
reads: 'Mr Adam Smith, LLD and FRS' and smaller, 'Professor of
Moral Philosophy, University of Glasgow'. He opens the folio to
the first page, mutters to himself, squints into the auditorium.*

SMITH (*pronounced Scottish accent*). Lights, please?

*The house lights dim. He clears his throat, produces a small
atomiser, administers two squirts to his tonsils, clears throat
again, then:*

Chapter One.

*Thunder, lightning, darkness. We hear a thin tune played on a
Native American flute. Out of the darkness, a* MOHEGAN
BRAVE *steps into a shaft of moonlight. He assumes a series of
ritual postures as* SMITH *relates the following:*

The Mohegan people of present-day Massachusetts believed
their forefather to be a benevolent giant whose wife was a
spirit of the trees, and that thunder and lightning were the result
of the married couple quarrelling in the sky. At the approach of
a thunderstorm, they would beseech these magical ancestors to
restore peace to the heavens and bestow blessings upon
themselves and their grandchildren. Of course, as we now
know, such blessings would never come to pass. Quite the
reverse; their descendants were to be placed in internment
camps and, in subsequent generations, work in gambling
casinos and sell discount cigarettes.

The BRAVE *hears a noise from offstage and pulls a knife from
his waist. A gunshot rings out. The* BRAVE *drops dead and the
flute music stops.*

This particular narrative, however, does not concern them.

A SHADOWY FIGURE *in a cloak and broad-brimmed hat steps out of the shadows, smoking pistol in one hand. In the other, a covered basket.*

Nor does it concern this man, though he will come to play a dramatic role in its unfolding some minutes from now.

The SHADOWY FIGURE *places the basket in front of a wooden door, knocks, and exits again. The door opens to reveal* MRS TRUMPETT, *candle in hand, with* PEG, *a prostitute, and* OLD ONE-EYED TIZZY, *a hunchbacked African slave.* MRS TRUMPETT *kneels to inspect the basket, extracting a letter.*

Rather, it is with regard to the individual within this basket that we shall confine the account, and the course of encounters that would determine his education, his progress and his eventual undoing.

Another rumble of thunder. A title reads: 'WESTERN MASSACHUSETTS, 1759'. From the basket, the cries of an infant.

MRS TRUMPETT (*reading letter*). 'To whomsoever Providence and I have delivered this bastard child: Circumstances force me to beg you care for him and bring him into manhood and should you be good enough to do so, in his seventeenth year you shall find yourself generously compensated.' Signed 'G. Washington of Virginia'.

She picks up the basket as SMITH *speaks.*

SMITH. The woman was called Dorothy Trumpett, or Dolly to some. And as she had none of her own, and reasoning correctly that the child would occupy but a tenth the space of an adult and consume correspondingly little –

PEG (*to* MRS TRUMPETT). Shall we bring him in, then?

SMITH. – she took him in, as she'd taken in the girls of her establishment before him.

MRS TRUMPETT. But only fer the night.

Festive music as we move inside what is clearly a brothel. PROSTITUTES *in petticoats dance with* OLD MEN *and drunken* BRITISH REGULARS. *A half-naked* PROSTITUTE *screams as a* SOLDIER *chases her through the room.* MRS TRUMPETT *sits with the baby as* SMITH *continues.*

SMITH. The tavern in which she conducted her business stood conveniently upon a crossroads, and as the ladies within had no marketable skills to speak of, they set about to purvey the only commodity available to them.

The music and debauchery conclude and the baby grows quiet as lights change to morning and birds begin to chirp. Others exit, leaving only MRS TRUMPETT *and* TIZZY *behind with* GUNNERY SGT. MANLEY *face down on a table.*

Mrs Trumpett sat 'til morning with the child. But milk to soothe its hunger was not to be had, as cattle were scarce and even swine a luxury. And thus, lacking other recourse, she husbanded the labour of bees to supplement her income.

A door opens and a hungover REDCOAT *stumbles downstairs, fastening his trousers. He rudely tosses a pair of coins on the table.*

MRS TRUMPETT (*proffering a jar*). Pot of honey fer yer family, sir?

REDCOAT (*as he exits*). Fuck off.

SMITH. And she discovered that if she were to place the tip of her finger into the honeypot and from there to the child's mouth he would suck it clean directly.

The baby gurgles. A title reads: 'WHAT THE WIDOW TRUMPETT FORECAST FOR THE BASTARD CHILD'.

MRS TRUMPETT (*to the infant*). Shhh… What a greedy little fella y'are. Greedy, greedy, wee fella with no manners at all. But you'll grow up to be a gent some day, won't ya? *Oh yes ya will!* A right gent with servants to serve ya and shine the brass buckles on your best boots, and you'll sit at yer table in the biggest house in town and dine on beefsteak and partridges and wear a pointed hat with a feather sticking outta the top, and you'll sit atop the best white horse and ev'ry time ya ride past folks will look up and say *what a fine gent he is.*

TIZZY hobbles up on her cane, smoking a clay pipe.

SMITH. But not all in the household were in agreement as to his destiny.

TIZZY (*Caribbean accent*). Can't come to no good.

SMITH *exits*.

MRS TRUMPETT. What can't?

TIZZY. 'Tiz a *bad* child, miz.

MRS TRUMPETT. What an awful thing to say.

TIZZY. Somtin' 'bout him.

MRS TRUMPETT. How could there be any fault in a dear wee baby?

TIZZY. Got hisself the mark.

MRS TRUMPETT. What mark?

TIZZY. Seen it dere on his backside. Iz a perfeckly round spot like a copper penny been fastened direckly to his rump.

MRS TRUMPETT. P'raps it portends a great fortune.

TIZZY. Nooo. Somtin' wrong with dat child.

A door opens and CAPTAIN SHIRLEY – *tall, brisk, polite, English, swagger, stick in hand – enters, sits next to* MRS TRUMPETT.

SHIRLEY. Morning.

MRS TRUMPETT. Morning, sir. I trust you slept well?

SHIRLEY. Tolerably well – if not altogether soundly.

MRS TRUMPETT. Tizzy, fetch tea fer the commander.

SHIRLEY. With sugar, please?

MRS TRUMPETT. Will honey do?

SHIRLEY. If need be.

MRS TRUMPETT. 'Twas such a rain we had last night I hope we kept ya dry.

SHIRLEY. Passably dry, though I must report the *bedding* falls something short of hygienic.

MRS TRUMPETT. I'll give 'em a wash.

SHIRLEY. But if I might speak to you on an unrelated matter – (*To* MANLEY.) look sharp, Sergeant.

SHIRLEY *pokes* MANLEY.

MANLEY (*awaking with a start*). Aye, sir.

MRS TRUMPETT (*to* TIZZY). And tea fer the sergeant as well.

SHIRLEY. Now, Mrs Trumpett. I'm sure I don't need to tell you we live in contentious times.

MRS TRUMPETT. O, I *know*.

SHIRLEY. I mean, here we are doing our level best to conclude this business with the bloody French, while at the same time the lack of hospitality my fellows receive in the cities is positively scandalous.

MRS TRUMPETT. O, it's *true*.

SHIRLEY. And I'd like to know on whose behalf they suppose we're fighting?

MRS TRUMPETT. What a shame.

SHIRLEY. I mean, we all kneel before the same sovereign, don't we? So what is to be gained from disparaging the very fellows who are here to look after your interests?

MRS TRUMPETT. 'Tain't right.

SHIRLEY. The *larger* point being that, what with the prevailing sentiments in town and the scarcity of alternatives, I'm afraid I must ask you to quarter another dozen of my officers in your outlying buildings.

MRS TRUMPETT. But – there ain't no room, sir – (*Continues.*)

SHIRLEY (*overlapping*). Mmmmyes. I'm sure you'll find a way.

PEG – *the prostitute from earlier – has entered, and timidly sidled up to* SHIRLEY.

MRS TRUMPETT. – we already got nine of 'em in the cellar and four more in the –

SHIRLEY. Well, we can hardly have the officers' rank lying about in the rain, can we? (*Seeing* PEG.) What's this?

PEG (*clears throat, then, in a small voice*). You ain't paid me.

SHIRLEY. Hm? Couldn't hear.

MRS TRUMPETT. Not now, Peg.

PEG. But he ain't paid, miz.

MANLEY (*to* PEG, *cockney accent*). *Shut up.*

SHIRLEY (*to* MANLEY). Steady on, Sergeant. (*To* PEG.) What's your name, child?

PEG (*in a small voice*). It's Peg.

SHIRLEY. Ah, yes.

PEG. I'm the one what sucked your cock last night.

SHIRLEY. And a cracking job you did of it. But: I *am* having a *bit* of a chat –

MRS TRUMPETT (*to* PEG). We'll settle it later, dear.

PEG. Why izzit they don't *pay* like the others, miz? 'Tain't right.

MANLEY *roughly shoves* PEG *to the ground.*

MANLEY. *Shut it, ya bitch.*

SHIRLEY (*to* MANLEY). Now, see here. We'll have none of that.

MANLEY. Aye, sir.

PEG *creeps meekly away as the others continue without pausing.*

MRS TRUMPETT. It's just my girls ain't been paid in two months, and they got so little to eat – (*Continues.*)

SHIRLEY (*overlapping*). Mmmyes, it's a difficult time.

MRS TRUMPETT. – and you know why they gets angry, it's cuz yer countrymen won't take none o' their paper money exceptin' to pay our taxes –

SHIRLEY (*peremptory*). Well, we all have to pay our taxes, don't we? Otherwise there'd be no militia to protect you.

MRS TRUMPETT. But who is it we's being protected from?

SHIRLEY. Why, agitators and insurrectionists.

MRS TRUMPETT. But... it's *you* they agitate against.

SHIRLEY (*with a sigh*). Oh dear.

MRS TRUMPETT. Cuz you don't *pay* no taxes, do ya?

SHIRLEY. Mrs Trumpett. You provide commendable service to my men and in return we provide you with protection. Now, surely that's a fair exchange, yes?

MRS TRUMPETT. But –

The baby cries.

SHIRLEY. And if you don't mind my saying it, *in* a trade such as yours, given the disapproval of your less permissive countrymen, 'twould hardly seem prudent to be *without* protection.

MRS TRUMPETT. But – but – but – as long as we don't got –

SHIRLEY (*standing, dismissively*). Yes, yes. Manley?

MANLEY. Aye, sir.

SHIRLEY. If you'd muster the fellows?

MANLEY *salutes, exits.*

(*Re: the baby.*) And who's this obstreperous young lad?

MRS TRUMPETT. Erm –

SHIRLEY. One of the girls', is it?

MRS TRUMPETT. He's... erm – (*Turns to* TIZZY.)

TIZZY (*improvising*). It's called Jim.

MRS TRUMPETT (*to* TIZZY). Jim?

SHIRLEY. *Jim*, you say?

TIZZY. Jim.

SHIRLEY (*to the child*). Ah, Jim.

MRS TRUMPETT (*fondly, to the baby*). *Jim.*

SHIRLEY. Prodigious *lung* capacity.

MRS TRUMPETT. Cuz he's hungry.

SHIRLEY (*to infant* JIM). You denied me a full night's sleep, my boy.

MRS TRUMPETT (*showing the baby to* SHIRLEY). But don't he got the look of a gent about him? I told him how he's going to be a proper gentleman some day.

SHIRLEY (*dubious*). Mmmyes.

MRS TRUMPETT. With a white horse and a feather in his cap!

SHIRLEY. Erm. Not to put *too* fine a point – *has* he property, then?

MRS TRUMPETT. Has he – ?

SHIRLEY. That is to say, inasmuch as a fellow is *lacking* in property – or the pecuniary equivalent – 'twould be something of an exaggeration to call oneself a gentleman. Feathered cap *or no*.

MRS TRUMPETT. Erm – He ain't got property *at* present.

SHIRLEY (*satisfied*). Well, there we are, then.

MRS TRUMPETT (*improvising*). But he'll *inherit* it.

SHIRLEY. A *legacy*, has he? And where might be the father?

MRS TRUMPETT. Virginia.

SHIRLEY. Splendid.

MRS TRUMPETT. He's a man of breeding.

SHIRLEY. Is he now? A pedigree! And has the fellow a name?

TIZZY. Washington.

SHIRLEY (*cocking an ear*). – Say again?

MRS TRUMPETT. Mister G. Washington?

SHIRLEY (*dubious*). *George* Washington, is it?

MRS TRUMPETT. Very like.

SHIRLEY. Of *Virginia*?

MRS TRUMPETT. Do you know him, sir?

SHIRLEY. Well – By reputation.

MRS TRUMPETT. And he's a man of breeding?

SHIRLEY. He's a man of many – He's a *tall* fellow.

MRS TRUMPETT. And has he property?

SHIRLEY. Oh, I should say. Some threescore acres in tobacco, as I hear.

MRS TRUMPETT (*avidly*). Then he's a man of fortune?

SHIRLEY. Well, his fortunes may have somewhat declined since – I say, are you *quite* sure of this?

MRS TRUMPETT. Oh, he's the father, sir.

TIZZY. We got a letter.

MRS TRUMPETT. With a signature.

TIZZY. Mister G. Washington.

MRS TRUMPETT. Of Virginia.

SHIRLEY (*sotto*). Then *might* I suggest we keep this bit between us, shall we, as the man is something allied to our mutual cause – ?

MRS TRUMPETT. Is he now?

SHIRLEY. – and to go spreading slander might not redound to our credit.

MRS TRUMPETT. Ohhhhhh, aye.

SHIRLEY. I mean – (*With a laugh.*) suppose all the bastards we got were to come knocking at our doors demanding recognition? 'Twould scarcely leave time to fight a war.

MRS TRUMPETT. 'Twill be our secret.

SHIRLEY. Well, this has all been good fun. And do see to the men's lodging.

MRS TRUMPETT. Pot of honey, sir?

SHIRLEY (*as he exits*). Heavens, no. (*Calling off.*) Sergeant?

SHIRLEY *exits. The baby cries.*

MRS TRUMPETT. Threescore acres! Didja hear, Tizzy?

TIZZY. In *tobacco.*

MRS TRUMPETT (*cooing to the baby*). *And who's the greedy boy who's to get alla that, hmm? Who's that greedy baby boy?*

Music. SMITH *returns as* MRS TRUMPETT *and* TIZZY *exit and* YOUNG JIM – *age six – appears. He holds something behind his back. A title reads '1765'.*

SMITH. The child's identity was kept secret. And Mrs Trumpett educated him as best she could. But he shewed little aptitude for letters, and far less for poetry or music, history or scientific inquiry. 'Twas only for mathematics he demonstrated curiosity, for at an early age he recognised the simple fact that whosoever has two apples is universally happier than he that has one, and that possession of the greatest number of apples equals the greatest happiness.

YOUNG JIM *turns and we see a hatchet behind his back. Behind him, a small tree lies upon its side.* MRS TRUMPETT *confronts him,* TIZZY *next to her.* SMITH *exits again.*

MRS TRUMPETT. Now, Jim, I want to know who it was cut down this crab-apple tree and I want the truth, now. Was it you, then?

YOUNG JIM *stares implacably.*

Cuz, there weren't no wind today. And that trunk there is as thick as my ankle, and bears the scars of a hatchet, so it don't seem likely it fell by itself.

TIZZY. Iz a bad child.

MRS TRUMPETT. Hush, Tizzy. (*To* YOUNG JIM.) Have ya no answer fer me?

YOUNG JIM (*beat, simply*). A nigger done it.

MRS TRUMPETT (*with dismay*). Why, Jim Trumpett.

YOUNG JIM. Honest.

MRS TRUMPETT. You know that's not right. You know what's wrong with what you said, don't ya?

> YOUNG JIM *nods*.

> What you *mean* to say is… a nigger *did* it.

YOUNG JIM. Yes'm.

MRS TRUMPETT. Not *done*.

YOUNG JIM. Yes'm.

MRS TRUMPETT. You know how to talk right.

YOUNG JIM. But he *did*. He come running out of them –

MRS TRUMPETT. *Came*.

YOUNG JIM. – came running outta them bushes –

MRS TRUMPETT. *Those*.

YOUNG JIM. – those bushes right yonder.

MRS TRUMPETT (*to* YOUNG JIM). And is that the hatchet he used? Behind yer back? Cuz that's *my* hatchet.

TIZZY (*re:* YOUNG JIM). I seen him trying to get at that apple and when he couldn't reach it he come back with that hatchet and that's when I come to fetch ya.

MRS TRUMPETT (*to* YOUNG JIM). Ya hear that buzzing, don't ya? That's cuz them bees is angry at us. Cuz without that tree there's no blossoms, and without blossoms they can't make no honey, and without honey then what shall we do come wintertime when we got nothing to shew fer ourselves?

> *During the previous, two* FOOTMEN *have entered at a distance, carrying a sedan chair. An elegant young Scottish gentleman – the* DUKE OF BUCCLEUCH *– steps out. He is impeccably dressed, a pheasant plume in his hat.*

DUKE OF BUCCLEUCH (*from a distance*). I say?

MRS TRUMPETT. And all because you wouldn't share a single crab apple.

DUKE OF BUCCLEUCH. My dear woman?

MRS TRUMPETT *curtsies and approaches the* DUKE. *We hear* SMITH:

SMITH (*voice-over*). It was to happen, on this particular evening, that a passing carriage would lose a wheel-rim to a muddy crevice. And, with darkness approaching and the travellers in need of lodging, Mrs Trumpett surrendered her bed for the sake of two gentlemen while she herself was obliged to sleep in the woodshed.

A tiny bedroom. The DUKE *hangs his hat by the door and sits at a table to groom himself before a mirror. Another man sleeps beneath the bedcovers.*

(*Voice-over.*) Henry Scott was the fourth child of the Earl of Dalkeith, Midlothian, and consequently 3rd Duke of Buccleuch, travelling abroad for his greater edification in the company of a learned tutor –

A knock at the door.

DUKE OF BUCCLEUCH. Come.

SMITH (*voice-over*). – and, needless to say, unaccustomed to such mean accommodations as those Mrs Trumpett could provide.

MRS TRUMPETT *creeps into the room.*

MRS TRUMPETT (*grovelling*). I thought p'raps ya'd like a wee toddy, 'fore ya sleep. Jest a little brandy and honey is all, compliments of the management?

DUKE OF BUCCLEUCH (*without turning*). On the table.

MRS TRUMPETT. My husband, ye know, he died at sea – got his foot tangled in a codfish net – but he used to say to me, he'd say, Dolly love, there's always gonna be those has to ride about in fancy carriages when the Lord gave 'em two perfeckly good feet to walk across the dry land. But I would so love to ride in a carriage of my own some day and wave a hankie outta the window.

DUKE OF BUCCLEUCH (*diffident*). Well, provided the
  blacksmith is of his word, come morning you may watch as we
  depart in one.

MRS TRUMPETT. Might one enquire as to yer destination?

DUKE OF BUCCLEUCH. We'll straight away for the port of
  New Bedford. And thence, bound for Toulouse.

MRS TRUMPETT. O! *La Belle France!*

DUKE OF BUCCLEUCH. Precisely.

MRS TRUMPETT (*tickling the feather of the* DUKE'*s hat*). *Honi
  soit qui mal y pense!*

  YOUNG JIM *has entered with a covered bucket and a plate of
  cheese for the table*.

DUKE OF BUCCLEUCH. The boots by the door are muddied.
  I'll have them polished by morning.

MRS TRUMPETT. See to the gentleman's boots, Jim. (*To the*
  DUKE.) And are ya quite sure ya won't take a lass to share yer
  bed with? Or yer friend, there?

  YOUNG JIM *drops a cheese knife*.

DUKE OF BUCCLEUCH (*to* YOUNG JIM). *Carefully!*

MRS TRUMPETT (*meaning herself*). Or p'raps a woman of more
  worldly experience?

DUKE OF BUCCLEUCH. Thank you, we shall decline.

MRS TRUMPETT. Well, if ya should –

DUKE OF BUCCLEUCH. And my *friend*, to use your word, is a
  great scholar and I'll not have him disturbed.

  *The bedcovers are folded back. The man in the bed sits up – it
  is* SMITH, *in his bedclothes*.

SMITH (*to us*). The listener may be interested to learn that it is at
  this precise point in the telling that the life of your narrator
  intersects, however briefly, with that of our small protagonist.
  For the fellow under present discussion was none other than
  myself.

MRS TRUMPETT (*to* DUKE OF BUCCLEUCH, *ignoring* SMITH). I do so worry about the boy, ye know, iffin' it's fit place to raise a lad, cuz ya got to instill 'em with the proper values, don'tcha?

DUKE OF BUCCLEUCH. You may leave us now.

MRS TRUMPETT (*servile*). O! O! Mais oui!

DUKE OF BUCCLEUCH. See to it we're awakened at dawn, and no later.

MRS TRUMPETT. Avec plaisir!

DUKE OF BUCCLEUCH. A simple knock will do.

MRS TRUMPETT. Et maintenant, *bon soir, Messieurs!!! Dormez-vous!!*

MRS TRUMPETT backs out of the room, curtseying as she goes. YOUNG JIM *remains.*

DUKE OF BUCCLEUCH (*to* YOUNG JIM). The cheese is mouldy. Pray take it away.

YOUNG JIM. Aye, sir.

DUKE OF BUCCLEUCH. I'll have an egg and a chop, prior to departure. Likewise for my companion.

YOUNG JIM. Aye, sir.

DUKE OF BUCCLEUCH. And, boy?

YOUNG JIM. Aye, sir.

DUKE OF BUCCLEUCH. The proper expression is *Your Lordship.* Rather than *sir.*

YOUNG JIM (*beat*). You're not my lord.

The DUKE OF BUCCLEUCH *stops his grooming and levels his gaze at* YOUNG JIM.

DUKE OF BUCCLEUCH (*coolly*). Well, not of the heavenly variety, but in the terrestrial sense I'm afraid I rather am. And if you don't mind your saucy mouth I'll have you *and* your mother horsewhipped for this grotty little brothel.

YOUNG JIM. Aye, sir.

DUKE OF BUCCLEUCH. Your Lordship.

YOUNG JIM. Your Lordship.

DUKE OF BUCCLEUCH. Now, empty the pots and be done with it.

> YOUNG JIM *moves to empty* SMITH*'s chamber pot, as the* DUKE *stands and exits.*

SMITH (*from his place in the bed*). And as he considered the disparity betwixt himself and the man whose chamber pot he presently emptied, he wondered what it should be that caused such divergence of fortune. Surely 'twas not the want of labour, since this fellow's hands bore little trace of it.

> YOUNG JIM *begins to empty* SMITH*'s pot.*

> But amid this reflexion, as he was yet of awkward proportion, his elbow made inadvertent contact with the sleeping man's inkpot, o'erturning it onto a sheaf of manuscript pages.

> YOUNG JIM *upsets the inkwell. In a panic, he collects the ink-stained pages from* SMITH*'s table and exits the room.* SMITH *follows him.*

> (*Trailing behind* YOUNG JIM.) His immediate impulse was to conceal the evidence of his misdeed. But when he'd crept downstairs and held the papers o'er the hearth, intent upon burning them, something inscribed upon the first page caught his eye –

> YOUNG JIM *holds the page above a hearth.*

> – and thus it was he encountered the paragraph that was to form the canonical basis of all his future thinking:

YOUNG JIM (*sounding it out as he reads*). 'Ev'ry...'

SMITH (*prompting* JIM)....individual...

YOUNG JIM. 'Ev'ry individual...'

SMITH (*taking over, to us*). Every individual endeavours as much as he can to employ his capital in support of domestic industry. He neither intends to promote the public interest nor knows how much he is promoting it. He intends only his own gain, and he is in this, led by an invisible hand to promote an end that was never part of his intention. Nor is it the worse for society that it was no part of it.

YOUNG JIM *considers the ramifications.*

And how convincingly those words resonate within the ears of a child. For if the fruits of a man's labour may be enjoyed without regard to consequence, if every penny therein derived is to be his alone, to do with as he pleases, he will apply himself to that labour, and once his prosperity is thus achieved, the rest of the damnable world can stick it up their fucking arsehole.

YOUNG JIM *smiles.*

Chapter Two.

YOUNG JIM *exits, to be replaced by the fully grown* JIM, *who sits at a table, writing in a ledger, a lock-box at his elbow. He has become a blandly handsome young man of seventeen. Behind* JIM, *and with his back to us, sits a* GREASY-HAIRED MAN, *silently sipping whiskey.*

With the swift passage of eleven calendar years, his musculature newly firm and his heart withal, Jim Trumpett had grown into a rough approximation of that which – in our modern world – we know to be the most provident employment for a young person of ambition: in short, he had become, a *businessman.*

A title reads: '1776'. During the previous, MANLEY *enters and approaches* JIM, *who does not look up from his ledger.*

JIM. Girl?

MANLEY. Tilly.

JIM. She's got an abscess.

MANLEY. Gimme Peg, then.

JIM. Peg's got her cycle.

MANLEY (*quietly*). Fuck.

JIM. Millicent, Pansy, or Tish.

MANLEY. Tish.

JIM. Top of the stair.

Without looking up, JIM *rings a handbell as* MANLEY *pulls coins from his pocket. A door opens and a* PROSTITUTE *steps into the room, glaring at* JIM. MANLEY *holds out coins to* JIM.

In the box, please.

MANLEY *grudgingly drops three coins through a slot in the lock-box.*

And the pistol.

MANLEY *places his pistol on the table before* JIM, *who places it in a drawer.* MANLEY *exits up the stairs, as* SMITH *continues.*

SMITH. And owing to his cleverness, he was granted supervision of the affairs of the house. Yet somehow it seemed that, as his authority increased, the affection of those within had diminished proportionally.

Before the door closes behind MANLEY, MRS TRUMPETT *creeps in, holding something behind her back. She is dressed somewhat better than before, and there are signs of general improvement.* TIZZY *follows behind her.* SMITH *exits.*

MRS TRUMPETT. Jim?

JIM. Aye?

MRS TRUMPETT. Are ye not aware what day 'tis?

JIM (*not looking up*). Uhh... Thursday, I reckon?

MRS TRUMPETT. And what else?

JIM. The fourteenth of April?

MRS TRUMPETT. And what else?

JIM (*annoyed*). Aunt Dolly –

MRS TRUMPETT. It's yer birthday!

She produces a pitiful little cake with a single candle, as TIZZY *blows a noisemaker and places a paper hat on* JIM's *head.*

So I made ya this honey cake, which I know to be yer favourite – (*Continues.*)

JIM (*overlapping*). Ye shouldn'ta troubled –

MRS TRUMPETT. – and I sewed ya three kerchiefs with yer
   initials, on 'em, see there in the corner? And Tizzy made ya
   some stockings fer when it turns cold again. And she's been
   knitting away ever since the firsta Lent, so whaddya say, now?

JIM. Thanks, Tizzy.

MRS TRUMPETT. And I said to her, I said, Tizzy, it's not right
   that Jim should be slavin' away at them books on the one day
   of the year that's meant fer his relaxin'. So let's put down yer
   pen – (*Continues.*)

JIM (*overlapping*). I'm very nearly fin–

MRS TRUMPETT. – and we'll all join in sayin' hip, hurrah! Our
   Jim is seventeen today!

JIM. All… *three* of us, is it?

MRS TRUMPETT (*beat*). Well, the girls is busy.

JIM. Or p'raps they don't share yer enthusiasm?

MRS TRUMPETT (*feigning ignorance*). How d'ya mean?

JIM. Only that the celebration is somewhat scantily attended –

MRS TRUMPETT. – But – but – but –

JIM. – Not as I much care one way or the other, but –

MRS TRUMPETT. But ya know why they might be cross with ya.

JIM (*deep breath*). However I conduct our business, Auntie, is in
   the interest of all – (*Continues.*)

MRS TRUMPETT (*overlapping*). And *I* know that.

JIM. – and superior in all respects to your system of management.

MRS TRUMPETT. But awful complicated.

JIM (*patiently*). At the end of each day I retrieve coins from this
   box and at *week's* end redeem them for a bond. And the
   merchant upon whom I hold that bond employs those coins to
   trade for other goods – (*Continues.*)

MRS TRUMPETT (*overlapping, to* TIZZY). It makes my head all
   fuzzy.

JIM. – and upon successful completion of the transaction, the
   dividend is collected – to our mutual advantage – at his return.

   A FARMER *enters in muddy clothes, holding a pitchfork. He
   stands to one side of* JIM.

MRS TRUMPETT. And that's when they get their money?

JIM. *That* is when the dividends are consolidated and reinvested.
   And the more hindrances they place upon that free exchange,
   the less gainful the return.

MRS TRUMPETT. And I know that, but –

JIM. Wealth creates wealth, Auntie.

MRS TRUMPETT. Aye, but –

JIM. Such is the nature of *finance*. (*To the* FARMER.) Girl?

FARMER. Pansy.

JIM. Top of the stair.

   JIM *rings the handbell again and the door opens, a different*
   PROSTITUTE *behind it. The* FARMER *drops coins in the box*
   as MRS TRUMPETT *continues to* JIM.

MRS TRUMPETT. But ya can understand, can't ya, how 'tis they
   might start to wonder what it is becomes o' the coins they've
   earned upon their backs?

JIM. They are safely invested.

MRS TRUMPETT. But – it's *their* coins, ain't they?

JIM. And shall be again provided they are not prematurely
   withdrawn from circulation. (*To* FARMER.) Here?

   The FARMER *stops before exiting.*

FARMER. Aye?

JIM (*to the* FARMER, *re: money*). The price is *three*.

FARMER. *Three?*

JIM. Three.

MRS TRUMPETT (*meekly*). Three.

TIZZY. Three.

FARMER. Since when are it three?

JIM. As 'tis plainly stated above the door.

FARMER. 'Twere two and six last week.

MRS TRUMPETT (*apologetically*). There's been expenses.

FARMER. I'll have her on credit, then.

MRS TRUMPETT. Can we credit him, Jim?

JIM *consults his ledger.*

JIM. Uhh… As I recall there is yet an outstanding – (*Finding the page.*) Ah. He is beholden to a previous sum of fifteen shillings, to which I will add the additional three, payable the sixteenth of May, if that suits yer outlook?

FARMER (*to himself, quietly grumbling*). *Sonofabitch.*

JIM. After which, failure to remit the full amount will result in forfeiture of his milk cow – (*Continues.*)

FARMER (*overlapping, to* MRS TRUMPETT). 'Tis neither right nor proper, ma'am.

JIM. – and I have a signature to that effect. But if the cost is not to his liking he's free to take his business to our competitor.

FARMER. *What* competitor?

JIM. There is a tavern in Grafton – (*Continues.*)

FARMER (*overlapping*). *It be twenty-seven miles from here!*

JIM. – what offers a similar service at a lesser rate, though the price may something reflect the quality.

FARMER. And ye'll not be touchin' any milk cow of mine, ya hear?

MRS TRUMPETT. Of course not.

JIM. Or p'raps you could *pleasure* yourself upon your cow – (*Continues.*)

FARMER (*overlapping*). Insolent little shit –

JIM. – if you esteem it so highly.

FARMER. – Ya think me not able to give ye the thrashing ya deserve? (*To* MRS TRUMPETT.) Fer had ya thrashed him well and truly when he was small, he mighta learnt a shred of respect.

JIM (*to* MRS TRUMPETT). I shall refund his payment.

JIM takes out a set of keys and unlocks the box, removing the FARMER*'s coins, which he snatches back from* JIM.

FARMER (*to* MRS TRUMPETT, *grumbling*). Young man such as this, and with a war comin' on – Ya won't see no boys o' mine sitting idle behind a table countin' their pennies, fer when the time come, they'll be takin' up rifles 'gainst these English pricks – (*Continues.*)

JIM (*overlapping*). A man does *good* by doing *well*, sir.

FARMER. – as oughta any able-bodied young fella. And 'tis all I shall say to ye.

MRS TRUMPETT (*to the* FARMER, *as he goes*). How's yer wife, Ephraim?

FARMER (*without looking back*). Well enough.

The FARMER *exits, slamming the door.*

MRS TRUMPETT (*returning to the topic*). I only meant that the girls has been wonderin' –

JIM. The girls are well provided for.

MRS TRUMPETT. – but since *you* yourself got coins to spend – (*Continues.*)

JIM (*overlapping*). Am I to have *nothing*, then?

MRS TRUMPETT. – cuz coins is what the girls can hold in their hands –

JIM removes documents from his ledger.

JIM. Each of these papers outweighs by threescore what meagre coins I glean for myself, but if the girls wish to trade me for the monies in my pocket I will gladly do so, and 'twill be myself does profit from it.

MRS TRUMPETT. And *I* knows that, but –

JIM. There be some in this world such as us, Auntie, always fends for themselves, and then there be a legion of others always sponging offa us what's worked hard for the little we got.

MRS TRUMPETT. But –

JIM. And now here ya sit, in yer damask dress – (*Continues*.)

MRS TRUMPETT (*overlapping*). Thank ya fer the dress.

JIM. – sipping Indian tea from yer porcelain teacup – And have ya not always said to me, Jim, some day ya shall be a gent yerself?

MRS TRUMPETT. I shouldn'ta mentioned it.

JIM. Well, this is the how 'tis *done*.

MRS TRUMPETT (*beat, chastened*). Ain't ya gonna blow out yer candle?

JIM *does so indifferently.*

I'll fetch a napkin.

MRS TRUMPETT *walks away and, once her back is turned,* JIM *surreptitiously opens the box and withdraws coins, placing them in his pocket before locking the box again. The* GREASY-HAIRED MAN *watches from over his shoulder.*

SMITH (*voice-over, as* JIM *collects coins*). What he neglected to inform them, however, was that as payment for stewardship of their finances, he had provided himself with a secret stipend proportional to what he felt his services should merit. He omitted this from general discussion, though, for the ladies' needs were modest, and as a future gentleman, his were understandably greater.

MRS TRUMPETT (*to the* GREASY-HAIRED MAN). Will ye be taking a girl this evening, sir?

MAN. None fer me.

MRS TRUMPETT. Are ye sure?

MAN. But I do admire yer lad, there.

MRS TRUMPETT *looks at* JIM, *confused.*

Is it *Jim*, ya call him?

MRS TRUMPETT. Aye?

MAN (*to* MRS TRUMPETT). He's a great conniver.

JIM *turns*.

JIM. Are we acquainted, sir?

MAN. Not as such.

JIM. Your face is not familiar.

MAN. But I'll have greater acquaintance yet.

MRS TRUMPETT (*beat, then*). Is it a *catamite*, ya seek?

MAN. *Nay*, I am no degenerate.	MRS TRUMPETT. Fer he only takes the coins and keeps the ledgers, ya know – (*Continues*.)	JIM. There is a tavern in Greenwich caters to such predilections.

MRS TRUMPETT. – seeing as he's the one's got the head fer business.

MAN. Know ye the difference between a weasel and a businessman?

Small pause.

MRS TRUMPETT. The diff–?

JIM (*to the* MAN). Do I give cause for disparagement?

MAN. 'Tis but a riddle – (*Continues*.)

JIM. Well, at the present moment –	MAN. – what be the difference – ?	MRS TRUMPETT (*whispers to* JIM). *A bit free with John Strawberry.*

MRS TRUMPETT *secretly pantomimes drinking to* JIM.

JIM (*impatiently*). – between a weasel, aye, and a businessman?

MAN. One is a deceitful creature of low character what steals into yer home and takes what's yours under cover of darkness –

TIZZY. And t'other one's a weasel.

TIZZY and the MAN *both chuckle.*

MRS TRUMPETT (*not getting it*). Is it *two* weasels, then?

JIM. P'raps 'tis best a man withhold opinion of another's business 'til he's got sufficient basis for the judgin'.

MAN. I *admire* ya, son.

JIM. And had you pursued *your* business with the same energy you invest in your whiskey, you might have less cause for discredit.

MAN (*merrily, to* MRS TRUMPETT). Is he callin' me a drunkard?

JIM. You've called me *deceitful*, sir, and questioned my character – (*Continues.*)

MAN (*overlapping, to* MRS TRUMPETT). The boy's right – (*Continues.*)

JIM (*overlapping*). – so you needn't wonder at my reply.

MAN (*to* MRS TRUMPETT). – 'twoulda been simpler to call him a *pimp*.

JIM, annoyed, returns to his work.

(*To* JIM.) Fer' ya can dress yerself up and sit behind yer desk, it don't change the fact that yer naught but a common *pimp*.

MRS TRUMPETT (*offering cake*). Would ya care fer a bit of – ?

MAN. *And* a bastard as well. However ya comport yerself.

JIM (*heated, standing*). My lineage is of no concern – (*Continues.*)

MAN (*merrily overlapping, to* MRS TRUMPETT). His *lineage*?

JIM. – to you, sir, and should you continue in this vein I shall acquaint you with the exit.

MAN (*with a chuckle*). Little fucker. I saw ya sucking a whore's tit the day ya was born.

MRS TRUMPETT. Is it possible ya might be confusin' – ?

MAN (*to* JIM). Yer mother was a whore from Nantucket, boy. And yer father her most dedicated customer. And ya'd be with her today had you not split her lengthwise in striving to be born.

MRS TRUMPETT (*to the* MAN). But yer wrong, sir. His father's a man of substance.

MAN. Iz he, now?

MRS TRUMPETT. Mister G. Washington.

TIZZY. Of Virginia.

MRS TRUMPETT. We got a letter.

TIZZY. With a signature.

MRS TRUMPETT. Signed by Mister G. Washington.

TIZZY. Of Virginia.

MRS TRUMPETT *produces the soiled letter.*

MRS TRUMPETT. See fer yerself if ya doubt.

MAN. What need I t'see that what I writ with my own hand?

MRS TRUMPETT (*beat*). What ya – ?

MAN. *I'm* the boy's father, aye.

An exchange of glances.

MRS TRUMPETT (*confused*). Then… ya're Mister George Washington?

MAN (*beat*). Who the devil – ?

MRS TRUMPETT. – fer it plainly says here: Mister *G*. Washington –

MAN. The initial G, *aye*. But –

MRS TRUMPETT. And George *begins* with a G.

MAN. As do any number of names.

MRS TRUMPETT. But it's always been George to us.

MAN. Well, that be yer mistaking.

MRS TRUMPETT. And if ya be *not* Mister Washington ye can
hardly –

MAN. 'Tis *Washington,* aye, that portion I grant ya –

MRS TRUMPETT. Fer Mister *George* Washington is a *taller*
man –

MAN. *What the fuck do I care what sort of man he is if I be not
he?*

MRS TRUMPETT (*beat*). I – I – I – I – then what should the *G*
signif– ?

MAN. 'Tis *Gilbert*! Are ye satisfied?

MRS TRUMPETT (*wrinkling her nose*). *Gilbert?*

MAN. *Mister Gilbert Washington.*

TIZZY (*beat, then*). Of Virginia?

MAN. *O' course* from fuckin' *Virginia* ya dim-witted –
(*Continues.*)

JIM (*overlapping*). Mind you keep a civil tongue.

MAN. – I left the boy here upon this doorstep in the midst of a
squall some seventeen Aprils past with intention o' returnin' fer
him, and here I am, true to my word.

JIM (*to* MRS TRUMPETT). The fellow's a liar.

MAN. And he's got him a birthmark, if ye doubt me, very like a
copper penny, to the right o' his posterior. (*To* JIM.) And if
ya'd deny it I suggest ya drop yer trousers an' let us judge fer
ourselves.

JIM (*to* MRS TRUMPETT). Doubtless he learned these facts
from one of the girls, Auntie, and the pair of them will now
attempt to extort some monies from us.

MRS TRUMPETT (*comparing* JIM *and the* MAN). There be little
resemblance.

MAN. True, he favours his ma.

MRS TRUMPETT. And it seems to me that, were ye *truly* the
boy's father – (*Continues.*)

JIM (*overlapping*). – which he is not –

MRS TRUMPETT. – which I can scarce believe, but if ya *were*, that we was promised compensation fer his upbringing, which –

JIM. *Promised* – ?

MRS TRUMPETT. – I know I shoulda *told* ya, Jim.

JIM. For the raising of *me*?

MRS TRUMPETT (*to the* MAN). And if ya're truly his blood I think ye'd make good on yer promise.

MAN. Well, in the future I trust ye'll be more skeptical. (*Turning to* JIM.) Now, I'll make a proposition: ya could remain in yer present line o' work, and in two months' time be conscripted into service and cut down by a ball from an English musket, *or*: ya could travel the road with the likes of yer pa.

JIM. You're no blood of mine.

MAN. Now, 'tis not a life o' luxury. But what more need a man than a whore and a bottle o' whiskey and a warm place to void his bowel? All of which are to be had in ample portions in such line o' work.

MRS TRUMPETT. And... what line is it yer in, sir?

MAN. Sadly, ma'am, 'tis the thievin' line.

The MAN *pulls a pistol. Others raise their hands.*

So I'll need to relieve ya of what's in yonder box as well as all that's in yer pockets. And I'd be takin' the boy by force but he's fully grown and I'm not one fer a fight. (*To* JIM.) So the choice be yers, son. But either way I'll have me the box and if that seem less than equitable I'll give ya a portion once we reach the Connecticut border, seein' as how it's yer birthday.

MRS TRUMPETT (*tragically*). Oh, *Jim*.

JIM. He leaves us little choice.

MRS TRUMPETT. Aye.

JIM (*to the* MAN). I'll fetch the key fer you, sir.

JIM turns to open the drawer.

MRS TRUMPETT (*to the* MAN). O, I beg ya – Can ya find no mercy in yer soul?

MAN. Tragically, ma'am, such is the nature o' the world. But I trust ye'll live long enough to replenish them savings, and I, long enough to put 'em to good purpose.

Then, without warning, JIM *turns and fires a pistol –* MANLEY*'s – into the chest of the* MAN, *who instantly drops dead.* MRS TRUMPETT *screams, and* SMITH *enters.*

JIM (*simply, returning to the earlier point*). When were ya promised these monies?

MRS TRUMPETT. But ye *shot* him!

JIM. And ye would've taken from my kin without tellin' me?

MRS TRUMPETT. But – but – but – he said he was yer *father*.

JIM (*taking the dead man's pistol*). The man was a vagrant and a petty thief and the world is safer without him.

MRS TRUMPETT. And is he truly dead?

TIZZY. Aye.

MRS TRUMPETT. *Lord forgive us!* I know we's going to pay fer this – (*Continues.*)

JIM (*overlapping*). 'Tis nothing much –

MRS TRUMPETT. – either in this world or the next.

JIM. – and as long as none other were witness there be little to fear.

The door flies open and MANLEY *rushes in, half-dressed, the* PROSTITUTE *behind him.*

SMITH (*to us*). And as it would have something impeded his progress to stand trial for murder under testimony of an English officer, and in light of the discovery that he was owed significant monies by one Mister G. Washington of Virginia, Jim Trumpett made what seemed, in the moment, the only reasonable decision.

JIM *points the dead man's gun at* MANLEY *and shoots him dead. The* PROSTITUTE *screams and lights change, isolating* SMITH.

Whereupon, shovels were located and the bodies of the two
men placed in a single grave and come morning Mrs Trumpett
and the whores gathered to bid adieu to their young assassin,
who, as he climbed atop the dead man's horse, found himself at
a crossroads more real than metaphorical.

A title reads: 'DEPARTURE'. MRS TRUMPETT, TIZZY *and
the* PROSTITUTES – *with shovels – gather roadside to see*
JIM *off.* JIM *adjusts the harness of a black horse of some
theatrical type.*

MRS TRUMPETT. Now, Jim. Tizzy wrapped yer birthday cake fer
ya lest ye grow hungry. And soon as ya reach Virginia, I want
ya to say to the first man ye meet, say, I be the true and honest
son of Mister George Washington and when ya knock upon the
door of his homestead ya need only shew him this letter and say
ya've come to collect what's rightly yers, and then send along
whatever portion ya think due to them what raised ya, which to
my thinkin' would be twenty per cent or so?

JIM. So I will.

MRS TRUMPETT. Preferably in smaller denominations or
banknotes. (*Beat.*) Ya look troubled.

JIM. Nay, 'tis only that the road ahead does bifurcate and I know
not which way affords the swifter passage.

MRS TRUMPETT. O! O! Tizzy's travelled far as Charleston.

JIM (*to* TIZZY). And which of the routes is preferable?

TIZZY (*hobbling forward*). There be the High Road which runs
'round Mount Greylock over Hodge's Cross, past Queechy
Lake and turnin' south after New Forge, 'long the riverside.

JIM. And the other?

TIZZY. And a mile on to the left diverges the Low Road, 'long the
Eastern shore.

JIM. And the two become one again in Virginia?

TIZZY. Aye.

MRS TRUMPETT. And which is the lovelier?

JIM. I care not for that, but is progress upon one the more rapid?

TIZZY. If ya take the Low Road ye might save yourself a day.

JIM. Then, if the differences be minimal, I should take the one 'tis most expeditious. Farewell, then!

   JIM *mounts the horse*.

MRS TRUMPETT. But, Jim?

JIM. Aye?

MRS TRUMPETT (*as secretly as possible*). 'Tis only Thursday and as the gentleman upon whom our bonds depend shan't return fer a fortnight… could ya see yer way to leavin' us with jest a bit o' change – ?

JIM. Auntie, my travels take me far from places of credit and who can say what contingencies might arise?

MRS TRUMPETT. But jest a shilling or two?

JIM. I can give you eight pennies.

MRS TRUMPETT. O, bless ya, Jim.

JIM. But do present the bonds to the merchant.

MRS TRUMPETT. O, I shall. And godspeed ya, son!

JIM. Farewell, Auntie! Ladies, all? And onward to Virginia!

   Music. JIM *waves*. MRS TRUMPETT *cries, and the* WOMEN *wave back. The horse sets off – however such a thing might be accomplished, theatrically speaking*.

SMITH. He proceeded in a southerly direction and the air was fine and clear and as he rode he felt his spirits elevate, not so much from the climate, as from the knowledge that, hidden 'neath his hat were all the monies he'd held in reserve for himself over eight years' time.

   JIM *withdraws a purse from under his hat, satisfied at its heft. He reflects*.

But did he regret his deception in leaving the ladies with deeds he knew to be worthless, while his own pockets were heavy with coins? He did not. For, as they had no *knowledge* of his private holdings, they could be none the worse for their absence.

   JIM *puts the money away and rides on*.

The horse was spirited and the weather held, and in seven
hours' time, he had reached the port city of New London,
where he did avail himself of the commercial opportunities in
town – (*Continues.*)

A town square. TOWNSPEOPLE *and* SELLERS *mingle.* JIM
*dismounts and hands off the reins as the horse is led away. To
one side, a platform atop which stand five or six African*
SLAVES, *shackled at the ankles, with one particular tall and
handsome black man at the far end of the line.*

– for if a man would aspire to the role of gentleman 'tis only
sensible he should dress the part: to which end, he purchased
one coat of blue serge with a chalk stripe, suitable to the
conduct of business, along with a silken necktie and as an
extravagance, a proper gentleman's hat with a distinctive
owl's-feather cockade.

During this, the MERCHANTS *surround* JIM *and dress him in
his new attire, and continue to do so through the following.*

And thus outfitted, he undertook to provision himself for the
remainder of his journey. Within the space of one hour he had
acquired one proper English saddle, two smoked ducks, one
peck of green apples, two loaves of hard rye, one quarter hock
of salted ham, one half-gallon of cyder, and thirty-seven
ounces of ruby port.

The MERCHANTS *walk away, leaving* JIM *with an enormous
armful of purchases. Behind him, a* SLAVE MERCHANT *has
mounted a platform, ringing the bell as he makes his pitch.*

MERCHANT. *Negroes!!*

SMITH (*voice-over, re:* JIM). But, his procurement thus
concluded, he found himself considerably encumbered with
goods, and in need of ready assistance.

MERCHANT. *African Negroes!!*

JIM (*from beneath his load*). Beg pardon, sir?

MERCHANT. *Fresh cargo of African Negroes!*

JIM. May one enquire as to yer starting cost?

MERCHANT. Bidding starts at three hundred.

JIM (*to himself*). *Three?*

MERCHANT. *Suitable for all domestic and agricultural purposes!*

JIM. I'll give you a hundred for that one.

MERCHANT (*ignoring him*). *Certified clean of all tropical diseases!*

JIM. One twenty-five.

MERCHANT (*briefly stops ringing*). There's a fella dockside, son, sellin' a pair of elderly mulattos if ya be of limited resource. *Negroes!*

JIM. And a vendor across the river in Groton, as I hear, sells at a third yer asking price.

MERCHANT. Aye, cuz they're infected.

JIM. They're – ?

MERCHANT. That entire stock o' Negroes has got amoebic dysentery. (*Re: his own.*) Now, alla *these* carries certification of the South Seas Company, *and* come with papers to that effect, and ya'll not get that 'cross the river, son, but the choice be yers.

JIM. That it is.

MERCHANT (*rings bell*). *Negroes!!*

JIM (*moving to leave*). And such is the blessing of a free market that I may exercise that choice.

MERCHANT (*before* JIM *can leave*). What sort is it ye seek?

JIM. I'm looking for one can lift and carry a gentleman's belongings and follow his horse. But never will I pay three hundred.

MERCHANT. 'Tis not I sets the rate, son. Regulation says I cannot sell at such price as would depress the market standard –

JIM. Fuck the regulation.

MERCHANT. – But if you're not one hundred per cent satisfied, within thirty days' time we'll gladly exchange ya for another of equal or lesser value, minus wear and tear to the first. Is it a *first-time* purchase?

JIM. It is.

MERCHANT. Then might I suggest you start with one of our *pre-owned* Negroes. (*Indicating a* FEMALE SLAVE *with* CHILD.) Now this here was only worked two years upon a cane farm, and is thoroughly docile and I'd willingly part with her for two seventy-five.

JIM (*interrupting, indicating* BLANKE). What's that one?

MERCHANT. Not fer sale.

JIM. Why ever not?

MERCHANT. That one be deef.

JIM. Deef?

MERCHANT. As a doorknob, aye.

JIM. 'Tis little matter.

MERCHANT. And by regulation, I cannot sell ya substandard goods.

JIM. And how d'ya know he's deef? Supposin' he's counterfeit?

MERCHANT (*directly in* BLANKE*'s ear, as loud as he possibly can shout*). *YOU THERE!!!*

BLANKE *does not so much as blink, but another* FEMALE SLAVE *begins to whimper and cry.*

(*To* JIM.) Deef as a stone.

JIM. Two hundred.

MERCHANT. What good be there in a deef servingman?

JIM. You have a product and I chuse to purchase it, whatever its faults – (*Continues*.)

MERCHANT (*overlapping*). Aye, but –

JIM. – and if it be unsatisfactory, 'tis a matter the market shall decide.

MERCHANT (*interrupting*). A moment, sir.

> *The* MERCHANT *turns to the whimpering* SLAVE *and savagely beats her with his stick.*

> *QUIET DOWN YA FUCKIN' CUNT!!*

> *The* SLAVE *cowers and goes silent.*

JIM (*continuing undisturbed*). And how is any man to ply an honest trade if some fuckin' regulator sits an ocean away, dictating how best he should conduct it?

MERCHANT. Son, he were foisted upon me by a sea captain and he's unfit to serve ya.

JIM. Two and ten.

MERCHANT (*beat, checks to see he's not overheard*). Three twenty.

JIM. Ya jest now said *three hundred*!

MERCHANT. May one enquire yer name, sir?

JIM. 'Tis Trumpett.

MERCHANT. Mister Trumpett. I can see yer a discriminating fella so let's say this: three hundred *and* ya get a new set of iron shackles into the bargain –

JIM. Two thirty.

MERCHANT. – for a set of quality shackles and keys is worth ten alone –

JIM. Two forty.

MERCHANT. – So you tell me what ya'll part with for me to put this key in yer hand today.

JIM. Two fifty-five and no further.

MERCHANT. Two ninety.

JIM. Two seventy.

MERCHANT. Two eighty-five.

JIM (*holds up cash*). Two seventy-five, or I shall make my way to Groton.

MERCHANT. Minus the shackles?

JIM (*sighs*). Two eighty, then.

MERCHANT. My friend, ya just bought yerself a fine new Negro.

JIM. Has he a name?

MERCHANT. Call him what ya like. He's deef. (*Producing papers and pen.*) So I'll be asking ya to make yer mark jest here.

JIM. Aye.

MERCHANT. And here again.

JIM. Aye.

MERCHANT. And this.

JIM. Aye.

MERCHANT. And this.

JIM. Aye.

MERCHANT. And once more.

JIM. Aye.

MERCHANT (*handshake*). And 'twere a pleasure doing business.

> *The* MERCHANT *takes up his bell and leads the other* SLAVES *away.* JIM *and* BLANKE *are left alone.* SMITH *has entered to watch from afar.*

JIM (*to* BLANKE). Now then:

MERCHANT (*ringing bell as he exits*). *Negroes!!*

> BLANKE *remains staring straight ahead.*

JIM. Here we be. (*Clears throat.*) Erm – That is… 'Tis yerself I'm addressin'.

> JIM *adjusts his position.* BLANKE *slowly swivels his head to stare at* JIM.

(*Cordially.*) Very well. So. I'm called Mister Trumpett, and ya'll be sure to always – well, p'raps ye won't be addressin' me

direckly, as such, but as ya'll gather from this here document
ya're now mine to – I don't know if readin' be among yer...
faculties, but the greater substance is to certify – (*Continues*.)

BLANKE *looks away*. JIM *tries to communicate with the help
of gestures*.

– or rather, 'tis testimonial to the fact that I, myself, am now
your lawful employer. And should we differ in matters of
business 'tis my hope we shall always come to a mutual and
amicable... (*Beat*.) Do ya follow any of what I've...?

BLANKE *stares straight ahead, unresponsive*.

Aye. So, I'll be asking ya to gather up these here things, and
'tis yonder black horse ya'll need to follow behind. So.
(*Indicating*.) This direction, here. And... off we go.

JIM *exits*. BLANKE *remains, not moving an inch*.

SMITH (*to us*). Mister John Blanke, being thirty-seven years of
age, hailed from the West African nation of Dahomey, but we
shall have more of his story to follow.

JIM *returns, stares at the immobile* BLANKE.

JIM. Did ye not – ? These parcels. These here. These very –

JIM *sighs, picks up all of the bags and loads them onto*
BLANKE, *muttering in frustration*.

(*Almost inaudible*.) – *of all the tiresome and dunderheaded* –
'twill be incumbent upon me, then, to demonstrate even the
simplest – ? (*Aloud, to* BLANKE.) In *this* fashion, d'ya see?
'Tis understood? Aye. Then let us proceed.

Music again. JIM *leads*, BLANKE *follows*. SMITH *speaks to
us as night falls*.

SMITH. The sun was in decline, and the road ascended steeply, so
that when they had advanced a mere seventeen miles and with
darkness descending, they were forced to decamp to the
roadside to await the dawn.

*A title reads: '17 STATUTE MILES DUE WEST OF NEW
LONDON'. A moon appears through the mist. The glow of a
campfire illuminates* JIM. *Crickets chirp.* BLANKE *sits at
some distance, staring straight ahead, ignoring* JIM.

JIM. Well, this be agreeable.

He gnaws on a piece of bread, chews.

(*Satisfied with himself, to* BLANKE.) So yer deef, is it?
(*Shrugs*.) 'Sworse things to be. Sooner be deef than blind. Or
lackin' use of my legs. Or afflicted with a palsy. Now, where I
come from we got us a Negro's only got one *eye*, which from
her perspective'd be a net loss of fifty per cent, but to a blind
man 'tis a categorical *boon*. So, while 'tis true, ya got yer
handicap, and 'tis surely forlorn, 'tis much to yer credit ye
don't bemoan yer predicament. Fer 'tis my opinion it's him
what complains most loudly 'bout his fate that's the most
deservin' of it.

He drinks, wipes his mouth.

What's more, I once knew me a deef whore could take a man's
prick halfway down her gullet and she was well compensated
fer the talent, so never lament yer deficiencies to me.

He looks to BLANKE, *who ignores him.* JIM *waves, snaps to
get his attention.*

Hey there. Here to yer peripheral?

As before, BLANKE *slowly swivels his head to regard* JIM,
who holds up food.

'Twas a score of miles ye traversed. Are ya not of a mind to
partake of some comestibles?

He pantomimes eating to BLANKE *who, without responding,
swivels his head away again.*

(*Quietly muttering* BLANKE*'s response.*) Why, thank ya, sir,
that I will, and 'tis terrible kind of ya to think o' me.

JIM *pulls out a handkerchief and fills it with scraps as he talks.*

And there's another felicity. 'Twere highly propitious to come
into the service of such as myself. Fer 'tis my experience, if a
man does treat his subordinates in a courteous manner, that in
due course that courtesy doth become reciprocal.

He rises and approaches BLANKE, *offering the food.*
BLANKE *continues to stare straight ahead.*

'Twill do ya no good to deprive yerself. I intend to cover forty miles tomorrow and if ya mean to do it on an empty stomach 'tis only yerself shall suffer.

BLANKE *does not respond*. JIM *snorts*.

As ya wish. (*With a snort*.) Deef idiot.

JIM *bends down to place the food before* BLANKE, *who, in one swift movement seizes the pistol from* JIM's *belt and levels it at his chest*.

BLANKE (*in clear and cultivated English*). And now I'll have the key to these shackles – (*Continues*.)

JIM (*overlapping*). *The deuce!*

BLANKE. – and should you hesitate you'll most assuredly find yourself the worse for it.

JIM. *I – I – I – You lay down that pistol, ya hear me? Or so help me I'll –*

BLANKE. Your weapon is primed and ready, sir, and I have the clear advantage, do I not?

JIM (*recognising defeat*). *Sonofabitch*.

BLANKE. So: the key, then, if you please?

JIM (*beat, then quietly muttering to himself*). *Goddammit to fuckin' everlastin' mis'rable –*

JIM *angrily digs in his waistcoat pocket, flings the key at* BLANKE, *who uses it to remove his shackles while keeping the gun trained on* JIM.

BLANKE. Obliged.

JIM (*to* BLANKE). *And yer no more deef than I be!*

BLANKE. And considerably better spoken.

JIM. You was in collusion – you and that seller was both in league to deprive me of my monies, weren't ya?

BLANKE (*as he unlocks himself*). That fellow was taken in by the same pretence as you, and was on verge of reclaiming the hundred pounds he'd paid for me when it became apparent he might cozen you for thrice the sum.

JIM *brandishes papers from his pocket.*

JIM. Look here: you are my menial as plainly stated in these documents. And 'twill go less hard if ya now do kneel and beg my humble –

BLANKE (*calmly*). I'd sooner kneel before the hindquarters of a dog.

JIM. You are my *property*, sir! You are my *goods*.

BLANKE. Go hang yourself.

JIM. *Oh! Oh! Myself?* (*Laughs*.) I need but summon a constable to put hounds on yer scent and in twelve hours ya'll be swinging from a tree.

BLANKE. They'll not follow my scent if I'm wearing your garments.

JIM (*beat*). If ya – ?

BLANKE. Off with them, then, if you'd be so good?

JIM. The fuck I – *on thy knees*!

BLANKE. You may either disrobe or I will strip them from your lifeless body – (*Continues*.)

JIM (*overlapping*). *These garments is mine!!*

BLANKE. – 'tis all one to me, though they will lose considerable value if stained with blood.

JIM. A man's possessions – Ya' hear me? – are his sacred entitlement –

BLANKE. I have endured your prattle, sir, for the better part of an afternoon and have reached the threshold of my patience. I would as lief not perforate you, but so help me I *shall*, if I must, and without hesitation. Now, off with them, and no further complaint.

JIM *stuffs papers back in his pocket, angrily begins undressing.*

JIM (*muttering to himself*). *Of all the goddamndest cock-sucking* – (*Aloud*.) These garments are the rightful spoils of my own honest labour!

BLANKE. And which of us has laboured more *this* day, do you suppose?

JIM. And if ya so detest yer shackles then ya oughta done put up a better fight when they first come ta seize ya.

BLANKE (*re: his underpants, with a wave of the pistol*). And the drawers as well.

JIM. The – ? '*Twill leave me plain exposed!*

BLANKE. Aye, and further hinder your pursuit of me.

JIM *removes them in a fury. He will end up naked except for the hat on his head, covering his genitals with his hands.*

JIM (*struggling with the stockings*). '*Tis the most miserable motherfucking useless piece of godforsaken* – There. There. Is't sufficient?

BLANKE. Now the hat.

JIM (*beat*). *What need could ye have* – *?*

BLANKE. Cast it to the ground.

JIM. 'Tis but a *hat*!

BLANKE. 'Tis not the hat I desire but the monies you've concealed within.

JIM (*beat, then*). *Them monies is all I have of value in this world!!*

BLANKE. Then might I suggest you learn to value that which cannot be obtained at gunpoint.

BLANKE *snatches the hat from* JIM*'s head, removes the purse, offers the hat.*

Your hat, sir.

JIM. Fuck you.

BLANKE (*tossing the hat to the ground*). Indeed.

JIM. And yer whole detestable race.

BLANKE. Very good.

JIM. And may ya rot in everlastin' hell.

BLANKE (*gathering* JIM's *clothes*). And may you, in your naked wandering, chance upon a moonlit pond, and, catching sight of your reflection, take note what a thoroughgoing coxcomb you finally are.

BLANKE *turns to exit just as, from out of the shadows, steps a smallish, bespectacled, high-voiced* HIGHWAYMAN *with a bandana covering his face. He – or possibly she – places the barrel of a pistol to* BLANKE's *head.*

HIGHWAYMAN (*quietly*). Surrender your weapon.

JIM (*laughing at* BLANKE's *expense*). *Ahahahaaaa!!*

HIGHWAYMAN. And forthwith, lest I cleave a channel through your skull.

BLANKE *raises his hands and the* HIGHWAYMAN *takes the gun.* JIM *cackles with delight.*

JIM. *Hahahaa!!! My good emancipator!!* You've done delivered me from this black devil!! Let me salute ya, friend, fer yer true and timely service!!

HIGHWAYMAN *aims the second pistol at* JIM.

HIGHWAYMAN. *Stand well away.* And place your hands atop your head, fingers interlaced.

JIM *looks down at his hands, covering his genitals.*

JIM. What… think ya I possess a *weapon*?

HIGHWAYMAN. I'll have them in plain sight.

JIM. Whereabout should I conceal it?

HIGHWAYMAN. There is none here to witness your shame, nor have I the slightest curiosity. Now, up with them.

JIM (*almost inaudibly, muttering to himself*). *Was ever such an abundance of knaves in a single fuckin' nation?*

JIM, *with his back to us, grudgingly places his hands atop his head, leaving himself exposed. The* HIGHWAYMAN *tosses a canvas sack to* BLANKE.

HIGHWAYMAN (*ignoring him, to* BLANKE). Take this and fill it with his provisions. Ah-ah-ah. I'll have the purse. And I'll be taking the horse and saddle as well, along with the clothing, and whatever foodstuffs he doth possess. The liquor you may omit, but for the rest, place it in the bag, and be quick about it.

JIM. *Nay, nay, nay! Hold a motherfuckin'* – (*To* BLANKE, *re:* HIGHWAYMAN.) Look there. Have a look. That were never no *man*.

BLANKE (*irritated*). What say you?

JIM (*to* HIGHWAYMAN). Look at 'im. *Look*, I tell ya. 'Tis plainly a *girl*.

BLANKE *stops, turns to look at* HIGHWAYMAN.

HIGHWAYMAN (*beat*). I'm a youth.

JIM. The *fuck* you are.

HIGHWAYMAN. A beardless youth.

JIM. A beardless *girl*.

BLANKE (*to* JIM). Wherefore do you quibble at gunpoint?

JIM (*to* BLANKE). Can ya not see? Observe his shape and, and, and – (*Continues*.)

HIGHWAYMAN (*overlapping*). If you doubt my mettle, sir –

JIM (*pointing*). – and the feminine timbre of his voice!

HIGHWAYMAN (*levelling gun at* JIM). *Hands!*

BLANKE. What matter if it be an Ottoman eunuch? His bullet will pierce you all the same.

JIM (*mocking* BLANKE). Oh, oh, will ya let yerself be *undone* by – ? If not a *lady*, then at best a most mincing little – Look there. That's a small but unmistakable pair of tits 'neath his waistcoat.

HIGHWAYMAN. I need only squeeze this trigger, sir.

JIM (*spitting with contempt*). Fuck you, ya'd never.

The HIGHWAYMAN *fires a shot past* JIM's *head*.

Shit and hellfire, ya stupid bitch!

The HIGHWAYMAN *pulls another pistol from his/her belt and* BLANKE *returns to the bag.*

HIGHWAYMAN. And I've two more pistols at the ready, should you further provoke me.

JIM. *O! O!* Only, put 'em down like the man ya'll never be, and we'll see who's to be the victor!

HIGHWAYMAN (*to* BLANKE). And the hat.

BLANKE *adds the hat to the bag.*

Now place it at my flank and stand alongside that fellow.

The HIGHWAYMAN *flings the iron shackles at* JIM *and* BLANKE.

Now clap these about yer ankles.

BLANKE (*confused*). Who is it you – ?

HIGHWAYMAN. The both of ye.

JIM. *Ah, fuck it all!*

BLANKE (*to* HIGHWAYMAN, *calmly*). Good sir, while I commend you separating this dullard from his surplus goods – (*Continues*.)

HIGHWAYMAN (*overlapping*). You have to count of three.

BLANKE. – you must not mistake me for one such as this – (*Continues*.)

HIGHWAYMAN (*overlapping*). *One.*

BLANKE. – that does esteem himself according to the quantity of material *wealth* he doth –

HIGHWAYMAN. *Two.*

BLANKE (*locking his ankle to* JIM*'s*). – *Aye. Aye.* You needn't – 'Tis well finished. 'Tis done.

HIGHWAYMAN. Now toss the key into the darkness.

BLANKE *reluctantly does so.*

JIM (*almost inaudibly*). *Motherfucker.*

HIGHWAYMAN. Gentlemen, I thank ye both for your indulgence and may the rest of your evening be somewhat more profitable.

The HIGHWAYMAN *shoulders the bag and retreats into the shadows. We hear her/him whistle to the horse, then a whinny and the diminishing sound of hoof-beats. Pause. Crickets chirp. For a moment,* BLANKE *and the naked* JIM *stand miserably shackled together, staring.*

JIM (*a long beat, then*). I hope ye're finding this a pleasant evening's occup– (*Continues.*)

BLANKE (*furious*). *O, may we not, at last, have a moment's silence?* 'Twas repugnant enough I should be linked to you by contractual means; how much more so when the links be forged –* O, I *shall be free of you, I do swear it, if I must choke the life from you and drag your naked carcass 'cross the countryside.*

JIM. *– well, yer a black fiend and ya've only yerself to blame.* For had ya not accosted me for – And 'tis my *right* to ordain yer fate as I see fit, and ye'll *never* be free of me 'less to rot in a cell for the rest o' yer natural life.

JIM *and* BLANKE *turn to see, at a distance, a blind man with dark spectacles, cane, broad Puritan hat and long white hair –* BROTHER NATHANIEL PUGH. *He nervously hums the tune 'We Must Be Meek' as he slowly taps his way along until finally, just downwind of them, he stops, turns.*

PUGH (*to himself*). Queer.

He resumes his tapping.

BLANKE (*clears his throat*). Begging pardon?

PUGH (*brandishing his cane*). Ah! Ah! Keep your distance or I'll strike thee!

BLANKE. You are safe, sir! There's no threat of harm.

PUGH (*laughing with relief*). Oh! Oh, bless me! I – I – heard voices and pursued the sound, then trembled for my scalp to think 'twas the *red man*, lying in ambush.

BLANKE. You need not fear.

PUGH. And while this stretch of road is well known to me I have seemingly travelled in a circular path for nigh on – can you tell me? Be we within sight of a milepost?

BLANKE. I did espy one a quarter-mile back, but 'tis hardly visible.

PUGH (*thinking*). Then, if the milepost be so proximate, 'twould only be a matter of some four hundred and twenty-seven – (*Beat.*) Do I detect another?

JIM. That you do.

PUGH. And you're quite certain you're not those would seek to deprive a fellow of his monies – ?

JIM. If only 'twere so.

PUGH. – for this road is notoriously plagued with thieves.

JIM. 'Twas our very *selves* they lately so accosted.

PUGH (*to* JIM). *Say not so.*

JIM. *All* of my monies, sir, my goods, my *horse* –

PUGH. 'Twas *providential*, then, I lost my way. For had you not been here my proxy 'twould have been *my* life in hazard. Let me then embrace ye, friends, and call ye both my brothers.

PUGH *approaches* JIM, *arms outstretched.*

JIM. I – I – I – I – I – should forewarn you, sir, that I do stand before you quite –

PUGH *embraces* JIM *and as he does, realises* JIM *is naked, feeling about him clinically.*

PUGH. Ah.

JIM. Aye.

PUGH. 'Tis other than expected.

JIM. I am quite thoroughly naked, sir. And this fellow and I are here shackled together by our ankles.

PUGH (*beat*). Have I encroached upon an intimacy?

| PUGH. I ask not *reprovingly*, mark ye. | JIM. Nay. You misconstrue. | BLANKE. In faith, sir, I would it were otherwise – (*Continues*.) |

BLANKE. – in truth, 'twas the brigand himself –

JIM. – An effete little fellow.

BLANKE. – who did steal away with his garments only to leave us in this sad plight.

PUGH (*sadly*). 'Tis a very plenitude of scoundrels does infest this little world. Then let me be your Samaritan. We shall clothe ye and shelter ye and bring ye to the bosom of His benevolence.

Music: the humming of a congregation. PUGH *leads them away as some ten or twelve* MEN *and* WOMEN *enter in simple dark clothing – men in high collars and the women in starched bonnets. They carry benches and a long wooden table, laid with wooden bowls as they sing a simple hymn.*

SMITH. Brother Nathaniel Pugh was the presiding Elder of the New Light of Zion Colony of Waterfleet, whose doctrine compelled them to shelter the careworn and weary, and thus provided refuge from the night.

The CONGREGANTS *sing, in harmony:*

CONGREGANTS.
I will bow and be simple,
I will bow and be free,
I will bow and be humble,
Yea, thou like a willow tree.

I will bow, this is the token,
I will wear the easy yoke,
I will bow and will be broken,
Yea, I'll fall upon the rock.

Among them we now see BLANKE *and* JIM, *now simply clothed like the* CONGREGANTS.

I will bow and be simple,
I will bow and be free,
I will bow and be humble,
Yea, thou like a willow tree.

As they conclude, PUGH *takes his place at one end of the table. At the other, his bespectacled daughter* CONSTANCE. *Upon conclusion of the hymn, they bow their heads.*

PUGH. Almighty Father, we who are unworthy so much as to gather up the crumbs beneath Thy table, do beseech Thee welcome into our midst two travellers, who, like unto the Damascene, have been raised from the roadside and brought into Thy care. Vouchsafe them this day Thy blessings and keep them evermore in Thy sight. Inthenameofthefathersonand-holyspirit?

ALL. Amen.

The BRETHREN *takes their seats.* CONSTANCE *pulls out a small book and opens it to read.*

BLANKE (*to all*). And I do thank you for your hospitality.

PUGH. Nay, nay.

BLANKE. As well as for the vestments and removal of the shackles –

PUGH. 'Tis *we* are blessed in doing His service.

JIM *notices* BLANKE *taking a seat.*

JIM. Is it… all together ye'd have us, then?

PUGH. How so?

JIM (*re:* BLANKE). Men and ladies, and even – is your table so indiscriminate?

PUGH. All are welcome, friend.

CONSTANCE. All but the Indian.

PUGH (*introducing* CONSTANCE). My daughter.

CONSTANCE. Father is predisposed against the red man.

PUGH (*reasonably*). Only in that he inclines toward *savagery*.

BLANKE. And the Negro? Is he likewise savage, think you?

PUGH. No, the Negro is *somewhat* educable but, as he is brachycephalic, that is, having a flattened skull and foreshortened braincase, he is at an intellectual disadvantage.

CONSTANCE. Mister Blanke is a Negro, Father.

PUGH (*delighted, not embarrassed*). Is he?

JIM. My bondservant.

BLANKE. If the Negro is disadvantaged, 'tis his own failure to edify himself through the blessings of education.

A female congregant – SISTER ELIZABETH *– whispers in* CONSTANCE*'s ear.*

PUGH (*generally*). Friends, ours is a simple table, I'm afraid, but we do have boiled turnips and pottage and you may happily eat your fill.

CONSTANCE. We have a special gift today, Father.

PUGH. Say again?

CONSTANCE. We have received donation of a salted ham quarter. Might we bring it to table?

General enthusiasm from the CONGREGANTS.

PUGH. As a rule, Mister Blanke, we do abstain from butcher's meat, but if the gift be charitable, and if it please our visitors – ?

JIM. 'Tis pleasing, surely.

PUGH. Pray bring it, then.

SISTER ELIZABETH *goes.*

(*To* JIM *and* BLANKE.) 'Tis our especial good fortune to receive such gifts from local business or anonymous benefactors.

BLANKE. Very good indeed.

PUGH. I take it *you're* a man of business, Mister Trumpett?

JIM. That I am, sir.

PUGH. In what line?

JIM. Erm. My mother – that is, my adoptive mother and I – do employ a small company of – of – of young women in – in – in – providing relief to – to – to –

PUGH. Commendable.

SISTER ELIZABETH *brings the ham to table*.

JIM. – And what business is it for yerselves?

PUGH. *Our*selves?

JIM. That ye merit such publick generosity?

PUGH (*beat*). We have no *business*, friend.

JIM. Or industry, then?

PUGH. We labour as far as subsistence dictates we clothe and nourish ourselves.

JIM (*beat*). Nay – I meant only how 'tis ye maintain yer coffers?

PUGH (*beat*). We have no *coffers*.

JIM. But, for unforeseen – as safeguard 'gainst the future?

PUGH (*with a laugh*). 'Tis He alone knows our futures, friend, and they will be disclosed to us at the hour of His chusing. (*To the table*.) Is the meat toothsome?

General approval from CONGREGANTS.

JIM (*to* PUGH). But – but – but – even *He* as you say, would call it inadvisable to leave oneself exposed to – (*Continues*.)

PUGH (*overlapping*). Our ways are not for you.

JIM. – unnecessary – nay, 'tis your right to live as you chuse, but – but – but –

BLANKE (*to* PUGH). I think it admirable modesty.

JIM. – But supposing, let's say, that others should come to take your belongings?

PUGH. We have no belongings.

JIM (*beat*). No – ?

PUGH. Thus, no fear of losing them.

JIM. Or – in time of warfare, as is likely near upon us?

PUGH. We abjure violence.

JIM. But I mean to say, what *protection* have you from the – the – the – vicissitudes of – ?

PUGH. If it is His will we should suffer then we surely *shall*, whatever bulwark we contrive.

JIM (*baffled, with a laugh*). And *yet*: *were* you to undertake some simple manufacture, by which you might derive some small coinage –

PUGH (*with a laugh*). I think it unlikely.

JIM. – then might *I*, on your behalf, advance those same coins upon a merchant or two and generate a modest return on the investment – (*Continues.*)

PUGH (*overlapping, declining, with a laugh*). You are too generous.

JIM. – for if one's coins sit idle there can be no growth, and without growth there can never be profit.

CONSTANCE (*looking up from her reading*). All profit is theft.

Dead stop. All turn.

JIM (*beat, confused*). All – ?

CONSTANCE. Profit is the result of the unequal exchange of goods or services. And were an exchange truly fair and equal, *none* should profit.

PUGH. My daughter, Mister Trumpett, is a reader of *books*, and inclined to radical notions.

JIM (*to* CONSTANCE, *condescendingly*). Uhhh… any man may justly *profit*, milady, by fair use of his property.

CONSTANCE. And pray define 'property'?

JIM. Property is – is – is simply a man's *belongings*, held in *stock* –

CONSTANCE. For, those that preceded us upon this continent shared their possessions equally among them – (*Continues.*)

JIM (*to* PUGH, *overlapping*). The red men, does she mean?

CONSTANCE. – they had no conception of 'property'.

JIM (*with a snort*). 'Tis but a *fallacy* – (*Continues.*)

SISTER ELIZABETH *has returned to whisper in*
CONSTANCE*'s ear.*

– and if you think otherwise, I suggest you deprive a Mohegan
of his property and you'll find yourself facing the business end
of a tomahawk.

CONSTANCE. Father?

PUGH. Aye?

CONSTANCE. Tim desires to dine with us at table.

PUGH *heaves a great sigh.*

Why do you object?

PUGH. Because he is *disruptive.*

CONSTANCE. He disrupts because we refuse him.

BLANKE (*scooting over*). There is room yet to be had.

CONSTANCE. 'Tis acceptable to all?

Muttered agreement from CONGREGANTS.

PUGH (*weary*)....But only if he be docile.

CONSTANCE *nods to* SISTER ELIZABETH, *who curtseys
and exits.* JIM *returns to his topic.*

JIM (*to* PUGH). Sir: would you not agree that the Lord endowed
man with certain native instincts – such as the will to prosper –
as He did any of His creatures?

CONSTANCE. And a *civilised* creature *restrains* its instincts.

PUGH. Consider the admirable bee –

BLANKE. To be sure.

PUGH. – who labours in service to his insect monarch, as we to
our heavenly one.

JIM. My mother, sir, was a keeper of bees, and the bee is but a pitiful *drone*, entirely dependent upon the welfare of his companions –

PUGH. The bee is *humble* and *meek*.

JIM. And humility and meekness are the proper attributes of *slaves*.

POOR TIM (*from off*). *Add-a-boots-a-sleighs!*

SISTER ELIZABETH *returns, bringing* POOR TIM. *He is a large, mentally disabled young man, who maintains a moist, squinty smile on his face. He twiddles his fingers as he rocks back and forth – bits of straw cling to his clothes.*

PUGH. Good evening, Brother Tim.

POOR TIM (*in a sing-song imitation of whatever is said to him*). Gah-deebning Butter Dim.

PUGH. Welcome to the table.

POOR TIM. Belkum doo-dah-dayble.

PUGH. And how might you fare, this evening?

POOR TIM. How bayou veritas eebneen?

CONSTANCE (*beckoning to her side*). Come, Tim.

BLANKE. Is he… of limited – ?

PUGH. My sister, while she carried him, was kicked in the belly by a mule.

POOR TIM. *Kitten duh beddy-bye da myooo!*

PUGH. The injury precipitated her death –

POOR TIM. *Kitten duh beddy-bye da myooo!*

PUGH. – and we were charged with raising the boy.

POOR TIM. *Kitten duh beddy-bye da myooo!*

PUGH. Brother Tim?

POOR TIM. Butter Dim?

PUGH. We must ask you not to repeat us.

POOR TIM. Mustachio lottery peanuts.

PUGH. Y'are welcome to join us.

POOR TIM. Ya woke up ta jaundice.

PUGH. But not if you simply echo whatever we say.

POOR TIM. Banana few pimply eggo –

CONSTANCE. Tim?

POOR TIM. Dim?

CONSTANCE. May we be silent now?

> POOR TIM *inclines toward* CONSTANCE, *who strokes his head.*

PUGH (*to* BLANKE). He's partial to his cousin.

POOR TIM (*loud whisper*). Hat.

CONSTANCE (*patiently*). No, Tim.

POOR TIM. Hat.

CONSTANCE. Darling?

POOR TIM. *Hat.*

BLANKE. What does he say?

CONSTANCE. His hat.

POOR TIM. Hat.

PUGH. What hat?

POOR TIM. Hat.

CONSTANCE. A *new* hat.

POOR TIM. Hat.

PUGH. I know of no *hat.*

POOR TIM. Hat.

CONSTANCE. 'Twas a *gift.* Not at the table, Tim.

POOR TIM *quietly rocks and twiddles his fingers*.

POOR TIM (*rhythmically*). Hat. Hat. Hat. Hat. Hat. Hat.

PUGH (*rapping his cane on the tabletop*). *Tim!!!*

CONSTANCE (*to* PUGH). It does no good to *shout*.

PUGH (*to* POOR TIM). You've been warned, now.

CONSTANCE. Or *threaten*.

PUGH (*to* POOR TIM). You know what shall happen if you persist.

CONSTANCE (*to* POOR TIM). Shhhhhhhh.

CONSTANCE *gives* POOR TIM *a turnip to gnaw upon*.

JIM. Erm. The coat he wears – ?

CONSTANCE. Aye?

JIM. 'Tis oddly – 'tis blue serge with a chalk stripe?

CONSTANCE. It is.

JIM. 'Tis of some quality.

CONSTANCE. You'd have him in rags?

JIM. Nay, but –

CONSTANCE. Or naked, p'raps?

BLANKE (*to* CONSTANCE). But as to *profit*, dear lady: I do take what you say, and would but add there are those who do redirect a portion of their profits to *charity*, so divided as they see fit.

CONSTANCE. Why not an *equal* division?

JIM. Do all make equal *work*?

PUGH. All are *created* equal, friend.

JIM (*with a laugh*). But plainly *not*.

POOR TIM (*quietly*). *Kitten duh beddy-bye da myoooo!*

JIM (*re:* POOR TIM). I, for one, have a mind that can reason and do sums, whereas *this* simpleton has little mind at all.

CONSTANCE. For which you'd deny him?

JIM (*ignoring her, to* PUGH). Does not the Lord, sir, reward us in *proportion* to our labour?

PUGH. Yet we are equal in His *sight*.

JIM. And what is there in *equal*? 'Twas never my mother's wish I should be the *equal* of others, but that I should *exceed* them.

BLANKE. By what measure?

JIM. 'Tis only the knowledge I may lift myself *above others* does motivate my labour. And, were *you* to organise *yourselves* along principles of sound business, so that the benefits of competition might prevail – (*Continues*.)

JIM *turns to a nervous* BROTHER AMOS *at the table*.

– *you*, friend. You have worked this day, no doubt?

BROTHER AMOS (*with a pronounced stammer*). I – I – I –

JIM. And so I ask: would you prefer the fruits of your labour be distributed *equally* amongst your fellows? Or paid to *you*, in accordance with your *efforts*, to dispose of as *you* would freely chuse?

BROTHER AMOS *cannot form a response*.

PUGH. Brother Amos has been troubled with drink.

BROTHER AMOS. I – I – I – I –

PUGH. He o'erturned his rowing dinghy crossing a frozen stream and when his wife and daughters sank to the icy depths, he could not rescue them for his intoxication. Is't not so, Amos?

BROTHER AMOS (*sadly, affirming*). I – I – I –

JIM (*to* BROTHER AMOS). But none *put* the bottle in yer hand, did they? Whatever the tragic outcome? So why should they be beholden to thee?

BROTHER AMOS (*at a loss*). I – I – I – I – I – I –

PUGH. Brother Amos finds it easier to abstain by living simply as we do.

Slight pause. POOR TIM *babbles*.

POOR TIM (*quietly, to himself*). Kitten de beddy-bye de myoooo.

JIM (*turning to a* SISTER). You, sister: would you not take more pride in your labour if you could therein derive the means to elevate your station?

PUGH. Sister Comfort was violated at the hands of her own father, and conceived of his child.

JIM (*beat*). Nonetheless –

PUGH. He declared her possessed of a succubus, whereupon her townsfolk covered her in pitch and drove her into the forest with the child in her arms, where it died of exposure.

> SISTER COMFORT *begins to weep. A mortifying pause as another comforts her.*

JIM (*undeterred*). And yet – that is, I mean – notwithstanding the –

CONSTANCE. And what of Tim?

POOR TIM. Whadda Dim?

CONSTANCE. Would you have him fend for himself?

POOR TIM. Fanfare a shelf!

JIM. I – Could he not operate some piece of simple machinery?

> POOR TIM *rocks back and forth, claps.*

POOR TIM. Nimble pacheenery!

JIM. And if not, you were never the *cause* of his impairment. So why burden yourselves with providing for him?

BLANKE. Have you no compassion?

JIM. My *honest* instinct is one of *resentment*. (*Continues*.)

PUGH. Say not so, friend.	BLANKE. Thankfully, you are the exception.	CONSTANCE (*baby talk*). What an unpleasant fellow, isn't he, Tim?	POOR TIM. Wander a cinnamon!

JIM. – Aye, 'tis, and 'twas heedless on your part to care for one who could contribute so little to your livelihood.

BLANKE. Do you not share the world with him?

JIM. And I share it with kings as well, but what charity does the king for *me*? Or rather, does he *take* from my pocket and call it *taxation*?

POOR TIM. *Knacks-asian!*   CONSTANCE. *Shhhhhhhh*.

PUGH. Those who come to this table, friend, are *disadvantaged*.

JIM. And what advantages have *I*? I've come from *nothing*, sir, with *no* assistance. What are *my* advantages?

BLANKE. Ya're not a Negro.

CONSTANCE. Ya're not a woman.

PUGH. Ya're not blind.

JIM (*dismissively*). Nay, *fie on't*.

POOR TIM. *Hat!*

JIM. What fault is't of *mine* if others were created lesser than myself?

POOR TIM. *Hat!*

JIM. Wherefore must *I* offset their shortcomings?

POOR TIM. *HAT!!*

PUGH (*to* POOR TIM). *Enough!*

CONSTANCE (*to* SISTER ELIZABETH). Find his hat, sister.

SISTER ELIZABETH *curtseys, exits*.

JIM (*pedantically*). In the Afric' jungle, 'tis the lion takes the greater share of the kill, by virtue of greater *ability*. That is the law of *nature* which you shall never contravene, no matter what policy you'd enact.

PUGH. 'Tis one thing to admit the inescapable cruelty of nature, friend, but quite a different one to *encourage* it.

JIM. Nay, for… there is an *invisible hand*, sir, does guide our actions – (*Continues*.)

PUGH (*overlapping*). Say again – ?

JIM. – and: *if,* as you believe, we were made in His image, and *if* 'tis in man's *nature* to serve himself, then 'tis in fact *your* misguided *charity* does pervert the very system He made perfect – (*Continues*.)

PUGH (*overlapping*). *Our?*

JIM. – by thwarting that self-interest that would lead us forward.

CONSTANCE. To what?

JIM. To – to – to – to – greater publick – As says the proverb: 'The rising tide doth lift all vessels in the harbour.'

The anachronism arrests them all.

PUGH (*beat*). The rising – ?

JIM. *All* vessels, aye.

PUGH. And what is the provenance?

JIM. Why, 'tis Scripture, surely.

PUGH. Never *Scripture*.

JIM. 'Tis plainly written that, a rising –

PUGH. Daughter?

CONSTANCE. Father?

PUGH. Be this from Scripture?

CONSTANCE. Nay.

PUGH (*to the* CONGREGANTS). Find us this passage.

They all open their Bibles as one.

JIM. And if we take *ourselves* to *be* those boats –

PUGH. Nay, the *meaning* is clear enough.

JIM. – and the incoming tide, the general improvement in publick treasure – ?

CONSTANCE. But what matters the collective *elevation* if the boats remain of unequal size and far distant from another?

JIM (*with an imperious laugh*). Ask not of me. 'Tis *your* Book.

PUGH. Have ye found the citation?

CONGREGANTS (*murmured*). No. / Nay. / Not I. (*Etc.*)

JIM. The same book that tells us the Lord helps them what helps *themselves*.

PUGH (*beat, confused*). Wherever doth it say – ?

JIM. I – I – I – I marvel that you can be so little acquainted with – ?

PUGH. The Lord helps them – ?

JIM. – helps *themselves*, aye.

PUGH. Be this Scripture?

They all murmur again.

CONGREGANTS. Nay. / Not to my knowledge. / No. / 'Tis not familiar.

JIM. Give a man a fish and you feed him for a day?

PUGH. Aye?

JIM. *Teach* him to fish and you feed him for a *lifetime*?

Once again:

CONGREGANTS. Nay. 'Tis not Scripture. / I know it not. / No, 'tis not here.

PUGH (*to* JIM). Friend, the words of the Nazarene –

JIM (*laughing, victorious*). Ye know not yer own Book!

PUGH. He said: '*The poor have always been with us.*' *Those* are Jesus' words.

POOR TIM. Cheeses warts!

JIM. And what is the remedy?

PUGH. The *remedy*?

JIM. How to *eliminate* that poverty?

PUGH. There *is* no remedy –

JIM. Aye, we *have* the remedy, 'tis well at hand, when each man doth pursue his *own* self-interest – (*Continues.*)

PUGH. Nay, nay, nay.	BLANKE. 'Tis the most curious piece of reasoning.	CONSTANCE (*dubious*). *This* is your remedy, is it?	POOR TIM. *Zeff-in-dress!! Zeff-in-dress!!*

JIM. – and those that *fail* to do so rightly fall by the wayside.

PUGH. What He tells us is that our obligation is *perpetual* and *without end*.

JIM (*remembering*). Ah! Ah! 'Tis plainly written, sir: '*Am I my brother's keeper?*'

PUGH (*beat*). That was *Cain*, friend.

JIM (*re:* POOR TIM). And why should I be *this* fellow's?

PUGH. Cain *murdered* his brother. (*Continues*.)

JIM (*overlapping*). But why must *I* be obligated – ?

PUGH. – He *murdered* his brother and *denied* it to the Lord.

JIM. Why should *my* earnings be confiscated and parcelled out to – ?

CONSTANCE. And why doth it *vex* you so?

JIM. Because 'tis *theft*!

CONSTANCE. To take from each, according to his ability – ?

JIM (*theoretically*). If you were to take the collective wealth of a citizenry and redistribute it to the poor and indolent they would surely squander it within the year.

CONSTANCE. Then we shall do it on an annual basis.

JIM (*triumphant*). *Taxation!!*

POOR TIM. *Knacks-asian!*

CONSTANCE. And those that refuse, shall have it taken by force.

JIM (*almost losing his shit*). *And I call it theft!!*

PUGH (*calming him*). Friend –

JIM. And why should our countrymen be engaged in a struggle 'gainst this fuckin' – forgive my – 'gainst an English tyrant if not to throw off the foul yoke of taxation!

POOR TIM. *Knacks-asian!*

JIM. And if you would but lend me some coinage – mark you – in two weeks' time I could redeem them for bonds, and for a small fee, double them in value.

PUGH (*reasonably*). What you describe, friend, is *usury*.

JIM. 'Tis *speculation*.

PUGH. 'Tis moneylending –

JIM. 'Tis *finance*!

PUGH. – and Jesus *drove* the moneylenders from the Temple.

JIM. Well, then Jesus was an asshole.

PUGH (*simply*). Let us pray.

JIM. And had he *befriended* these moneylenders p'raps his fate mighta been different.

CONGREGANTS *and* BLANKE *bow their heads*.

PUGH. Almighty Father, illuminate our brother in Thy mysteries; that he may come to distinguish the value of Jesus' words from the value of money.

JIM. *Nay, nay – Pray fer yer own selves, not fer me, and the Lord'll tell ye to get offa yer lazy backsides and earn yer keep!*

POOR TIM *begins rocking and twiddling and quietly chanting throughout the following*.

POOR TIM. Cheeses and munny and cheeses and munny and cheeses and munny... (*Etc.*)

JIM. Fer what other purpose *be* there to *living*, if not to prosper and – and – and – What of your children? How shall they ever – Where *are* your children?

PUGH. We have no children.

JIM (*beat*). No – ?

PUGH. 'Twould violate our vows of celibacy.

JIM finds this hilarious.

JIM (*snidely*). *Yer* – Why, 'tis the most empty-headed – So ye'll *perish*, will ye? With no continuation of your blood, and naught to shew fer yerselves but a bowl of mouldy turnips and yer hollow piety?

JIM wipes his mouth and rises from the table.

POOR TIM....and cheeses and munny and cheeses and munny and cheeses and... (*Etc.*)

JIM (*as cruelly as possible*). Then 'tis my fondest wish ye may be stricken with a famine and find yerselves in need – Fer *when* ye drop to yer knees and pray to yer God, and *when* no reply is forthcoming and ye needs must go door to door fer *charity* – Then those of us what fended fer *ourselves*, then shall we look out our windows and *laugh* at yer distress. And 'tis then, I pray, the *true* nature o' things shall disclose itself to ya.

As he was speaking, SISTER ELIZABETH *has returned with a hat –* JIM*'s hat – and placed it on* POOR TIM*'s head.* POOR TIM *claps his fat little hands.*

POOR TIM (*in delight*). *Hat!*

JIM. *Give me that!!* (*Continues.*)

JIM instantly snatches the hat from POOR TIM*'s head and pulls at the coat from his back.* POOR TIM *throws a fit, hitting himself in the head with his own fists.*

JIM. – *'Tis mine, ya simple-minded –* (*Continues.*)	POOR TIM (*panicky screaming*). *Aaaaaaaagh!!! Haaaaaaaaaaaaat !!!!*	BLANKE. Why must you abuse this fellow, Return it at once, I say!

PUGH. What is this? Why the consternation?	CONSTANCE (*to* JIM). Why must you treat him so viciously? Unhand him!

JIM. – *And the coat as well!!* (*In a fury, to* BLANKE.) The *fuck* I will! 'Tis *mine*, as ya well know!! (*Continues.*)

PUGH (*overlapping*). *May we not have peace?*

JIM. – *As* is this coat, *as* is this salted ham!

JIM *grabs the platter with the ham.* POOR TIM *begins rocking and chanting to soothe himself.*

| BLANKE (*to* JIM). Why such ingratitude to those who've only done you charity? | POOR TIM. Cheeses and munny and cheeses and munny and cheeses and munny… |

JIM (*to* BLANKE). 'Tis no *charity* to return what ye done *stole* from a man.

PUGH. *We?*

JIM (*to* PUGH). Someone 'mongst ye here did relieve me of my goods this night – and if I be not mistaken – (*Re:* CONSTANCE.) this lady knows plain well who 'twas.

CONSTANCE (*merrily*). Oh, *I* stole your things, did I?

JIM. *And ya know ya did, ya thieving bitch* – (*Continues.*)

CONGREGANTS *all laugh at* JIM*'s accusation.*

| JIM. – *and gave them to one who, by the smell of him, lacks the sense not to shit in his own trousers.* | CONSTANCE. And how did I overpower you, sir? Through fisticuffs? | PUGH. This is no place for – May we not have a moment's – ? | POOR TIM (*increasing in volume*). …*cheeses and munny and CHEESES AND MUNNY AND…* |

PUGH *slams his cane on the tabletop.*

PUGH. *Tim!!*

POOR TIM. *Dim!!*

PUGH. *Confound it all*.

POOR TIM (*quietly*). *Gun fountain doll!*

PUGH. Fetch the branks!

> SISTER ELIZABETH *curtseys, exits*.

POOR TIM (*almost silently*)....and cheeses and munny and cheeses and munny... (*Etc.*)

JIM. I think ye're a parcel o' thieves and parasites and I'll no more of yer fuckin' 'charity' now I know from whence it doth derive. (*To* BLANKE.) Come, follow.

BLANKE (*calmly, from where he sits*). Who is it you command?

JIM (*beat*). I say we'll be gone from this place.

BLANKE. And I say go your ways. I'll nothing more with you.

JIM (*beat, calmly*). And I say you'll do as you're commanded.

PUGH. The fellow is free to come and go at his reckoning.

> JIM *pulls the recovered papers from the coat pocket, brandishes them at* PUGH.

JIM. This *fellow*, sir, was freely bought in the marketplace and if ye'd hold him 'gainst my will ye'll be owing me the sum of three hundred pounds as specified in these documents which I'd gladly shew ya *had ya the eyes in yer fuckin' head with which to read*. (*To* BLANKE.) Now, I say: on your feet.

BLANKE (*calmly*). And I say thank you, I shall remain.

> JIM *grabs* PUGH*'s cane, wields it at* BLANKE. *A struggle follows, in which two of the* BRETHREN *restrain* JIM *and the* WOMEN *shield* BLANKE.

JIM. *And I say get offa your fucking ass* – (*Continues*.)

JIM. – *ya sono-*	PUGH. Our Father,	CONSTANCE (*to*
fabitch or I'll	who art in	BRETHREN).
thrash you 'til you	Heaven;	Lay hands on
no longer have	Hallowed be thy	him! (*To* JIM.)
breath to – (*To*	name. Thy	You are
BRETHREN.)	kingdom come,	overmatched, sir,
Get yer fuckin'	thy will be done,	and would best
hands offa me!!!	on Earth, as it is...	own your defeat.

BLANKE (*to* JIM). You may talk yourself to exhaustion but you shall impose your will on me no further.

POOR TIM (*clapping his hands*). *Cheeses and munny and cheeses and munny and* – (*Continues.*)

The BRETHREN *fling* JIM *backwards, relieving him of the cane in the process. During the struggle,* SMITH *has entered to one side.*

PUGH....in Heaven.

POOR TIM. – cheeses and munny and cheeses and munny and cheeses and munny and –

But POOR TIM*'s chanting is suddenly interrupted as* SISTER ELIZABETH *locks an iron cage in place around his head, immobilising his tongue so that he can only make a gurgling noise.*

JIM (*panting from the struggle*). I shall return for what's mine. D'ye hear? Or what I paid fer it. Or ye'll regret havin' crossed me.

JIM *returns his hat to his head and snottily exits.*

SMITH. And with that, Mister Trumpett departed, leaving Mister Blanke to sit down before the hearth with the old man, who begged him recount the convoluted tale of his origin.

CONGREGANTS *remove the tables and benches and exit, leaving* PUGH *and* BLANKE *behind.* PUGH *weaves a cane basket next to* BLANKE, *illuminated by the fire. A title reads: 'THE STORY OF MR JOHN BLANKE'. Dulcimer music behind.*

BLANKE. I do but recollect a tropical setting and the sweet aroma of palm wine and a particular day when, being no more than nine years of age and having entered into a thicket I found myself set upon by a brace of mahogany-skinned fellows who beat me and placed me within a canvas sack, out of which, in three days' time, they deposited me onto a sea-coast within sight of a brigantine and her crew, who forced me below decks, where I received such a salutation in my nostrils as never in my life, and in this pestilential stench and darkness I descried a multitude of other dark-skinned folk in identical postures of abject misery.

PUGH. Grievous.

BLANKE. The following morning I was brought topside where my hands were fastened painfully to a hawser. So, to alleviate my misery, I sang a snatch of tune I recalled from infancy:

He sings, in Igbo:

Onye mere nwa nebe akwa.
Egbe mere nwa nebe akwa.

PUGH. Mellifluous.

BLANKE. And as I sang, I felt myself observed by a fair-haired man nearby, who looked upon me with sympathy, and by the time we made landfall in Barbados he had taken an especial interest in my plight.

PUGH. Fortuitous.

BLANKE. His name was Mister John Andrews, of Rivington, Lancashire, and when the others were discharged upon the shore I was redirected onto a schooner called the *Zephyr*, bound for Liverpool. And before we were within sight of the Mersey I had already learnt enough words to call him 'Father' and myself his 'ward'.

PUGH. Poignant.

BLANKE. But as in my native tongue there be an assortment of sounds as have no English equivalent, he chose to call me *John*, like himself, leaving the surname *blank* upon my christening page. From thenceforward, *John Blanke* would become my name, and Mister Andrews my guardian.

PUGH. Deliverance!

BLANKE. It was in my fourteenth year I made acquaintance with a certain girl, one Mary Cleere by name, who had likewise in her youth been plucked from Africa's bosom. She had a complexion of glossy chestnut, and we became inseparable allies, and in time the alliance deepened to, dare I say, love.

PUGH. Heartwarming.

BLANKE. But my benefactor fell ill of a quinsy, and as I sat bedside he looked upon my face and said, know you, John, that Rivington be without a male inheritor? And I told him aye, and

he said to me, then, as my favourite, 'tis my life's wish it
should be yours.

PUGH. Munificence!

BLANKE. Regrettably, none were witness to his proclamation,
and at his death, his daughter turned me out and, worse, took
especial pains to have my Mary sent abroad to thwart our
future happiness.

PUGH. Tragedy!

BLANKE. For some months I wandered Lancashire a pitiful
beggar, until one night when, having lain down in a hayloft, I
was freshly set upon and beaten into senselessness, and awoke
some hours later only to find myself again shipboard with an
iron collar 'round my neck.

PUGH. Calamity!

BLANKE. I implored with the captain, saying, I am the rightful
Earl of Rivington, and if you will but release me I shall give
proof of my tale. For these words I received a surfeit of
mockery and scornful abuse and was deprived of food until I
should recant them.

PUGH. Brutality!

BLANKE. For ten years' time I cultivated tobacco in the
Carolinas, and as many times as I attempted escape the master
would, upon recapture, sever another toe from my left foot as
punishment, as you will note by the disparity in my footwear.

He holds up his feet, the soles asymmetrical.

PUGH. Grisly.

BLANKE. Indeed, he threatened to remove the foot entirely, and
would have so, had he not lost me to a sea captain in a drunken
game of dice. For the last three years I've served shipboard
while feigning deafness, awaiting such time as I might return
to dry land and make my final escape or die in the attempt.

PUGH. Courageous.

BLANKE. And whatever the depths of my misery, I've always
dreamed of my Mary, and how innocently we played, and if

luck and Providence do favour me, some day we two shall be reunited, if not upon these, then upon some farther shore.

SMITH *addresses us.*

SMITH. Yet, as this tale was unfolding, what, you might ask, had become of our young protagonist? (*Continues*.)

Exit PUGH *and* BLANKE. *As* SMITH *speaks, a door opens and music spills out from what we may assume to be a tavern. A drunken* HESSIAN SOLDIER *in mitred cap stumbles out, full of beer. He carries a musket fixed with a bayonet and softly sings to himself – in German – 'Wenn ich ein Vöglein wär'. He unbuttons his fly to pee as* HESSIAN 2 *appears at the open door, holding a plate with a sausage.*

– To answer that question, we must move some two and a half geographical miles west of the present location.

HESSIAN 2. He! Was hast du mit meiner Wurst gemacht? [Hey! What happened to my sausage?]

HESSIAN 1. Was für eine Wurst? [What sausage?]

HESSIAN 2. Ich hatte auf diesem Teller zwei Würste! [I had two sausages on this plate!]

HESSIAN 1. Ich hab deine verfluchte Wurst nicht angefasst. [I don't have your fucking sausage.]

HESSIAN 2 *exits again through the open door.*

SMITH. For, as Mister Blanke was recounting his sorrows, Mister Trumpett had set out on foot to put some distance between himself and those whose philosophy he found so detestable.

Two other HESSIANS – 3 *and* 4 – *also with muskets – erect a gate parallel to the proscenium – a pole between two uprights.*

What he failed to anticipate, however, was that, as it was *wartime*, certain roadways would be subject to strategic blockade –

JIM *comes marching up the road in his reclaimed clothing, a large sack over his shoulder. He comes to a stop behind the gate.*

JIM (*out of breath*). I'd like to pass, if I might?

HESSIANS 3 *and* 4 *lounge against the uprights, one gnawing an apple, one paring his nails.*

SMITH. – and this particular stretch had lately fallen under control of a detachment of Hessian fusiliers in service to the English cause.

JIM (*to* HESSIAN 3). I say, would you be so good as to lift this barrier for me? Or would you have me go around?

HESSIAN 3 (*lazily, to* HESSIAN 1). Uhhh… Rolf?

HESSIAN 1 (*at a distance*). Was? [What?]

HESSIAN 3. Wie viel muss er uns zahlen? [How much is he supposed to pay us?]

HESSIAN 1. Frag Heinz. [Ask Heinz.]

HESSIAN 3 (*to the open door*). *Heinz!*

HESSIAN 2 (*from off*). *Was?* [*What?*]

HESSIAN 3. *Hier will einer passieren.* [*Some guy out here wants to pass.*]

SMITH. As an historical footnote, the road upon which they presently stood had been, in its primordial past, a dry stream bed trafficked by extinct reptilian sauropods, later by wolves and white-tailed deer, then as a footpath by indigenous tribal peoples, a bridle path by Dutch settlers, and finally improved for vehicular traffic out of necessity. It is known today, in its official nomenclature, as US Interstate Ninety-Five.

JIM *grows impatient and attempts to go under the barrier.* HESSIAN 3 *levels his musket at him.*

HESSIAN 3. *Na, na, na! Immer mit der Ruhe!* [*Whoa, whoa, whoa! Easy.*]

JIM. By what authority do you waylay me thus?

HESSIAN 2 *is back at the door, wiping his mouth with a napkin.*

HESSIAN 2 (*to* HESSIAN 3). Von wem redest du eigentlich? [What guy are you talking about?]

HESSIAN 3 *indicates* JIM.

JIM. Does not a one of you speak proper English?

HESSIAN 2. Uhhhhh – English. I speak, ja.

JIM. Then look here. This fellow has delayed me here on pretext of imposing custom on a publick thoroughfare, and I am in some haste to proceed.

HESSIAN 2. Uhhhhh – Ja. Okay. Uhh – It is here that you are needing to pay tax.

JIM *stares, blinking*.

JIM (*evenly*). Is it?

HESSIAN 2 (*indicates the palm of his hand*). Tax for road, ja.

JIM. I see.

HESSIAN 2. You pay to me now.

SMITH. The attentive listener may anticipate what is to follow.

JIM. Now listen well: in the past thirty-six hours I've been three times threatened at point of pistols, I've been stripped naked, deprived of my horse and the whole of my savings, I've been subjected to the insults of a blind, sermonising *pedant* and I am *fatigued*, sir, and will not now submit to your illicit fucking extortion.

HESSIAN 3 (*to* HESSIAN 2). Wovon redet der verflucht noch mal? [The fuck is he talking about?]

JIM. I am the son of Mister George Washington of Virginia, and when my countrymen send you packing back to the rat-infested continent from whence you came, you shall be free to pay all the fucking taxes you desire, and may the final one be upon your collective motherfucking graves.

HESSIAN 3 *stops eating his apple, thinks*.

SMITH. And if, in future, Jim Trumpett was to admit the possibility of having mistaken in any particular, 'twould likely be in having identified himself thusly.

HESSIAN 3 (*to* HESSIAN 2). Hat er *Washington* gesagt? [Did he say *Washington*?]

HESSIAN 2. *Sohn* von Washington. [*Son* of Washington.]

HESSIAN 3 (*beat*). *George* Washington?

HESSIAN 2. Glaube schon. [That's what he said.]

HESSIAN 3. Der *Virginia*?

HESSIAN 2 (*to* JIM, *suspiciously*). So… you are *son* of *Washington*?

JIM. The same!

HESSIAN 3. Huh.

HESSIAN 2. Jupp. [Yep.]

HESSIAN 3 (*beat*). Dann legen wir ihn wohl besser um. [Then I guess we have to kill him.]

HESSIAN 2 (*with a shrug*). Von mir aus. [Fine with me.]

> HESSIAN 3 *blows an extremely loud whistle. A drum roll begins.* HESSIANS 1 *and* 2 *grab* JIM *and drag him backwards toward a wall, where they fasten his hands and blindfold him. Two more* HESSIANS *with muskets enter, joining the others to form a firing squad.* HESSIAN 2 *pulls a sabre from his scabbard, holds it aloft.*

> *Kraft des mir von Seiner Majestät George dem Dritten verliehenen Rechts erkläre ich diesen Mann zu einem Feind der Krone, der sein Leben verwirkt hat. Alle dafür?* [*By the power vested in me by His Majesty George III, I hereby pronounce this man an enemy of the Crown and in forfeit of his life. All in favour?*]

HESSIANS. *Jawohl!*

JIM. *But you've not the authority!*

HESSIAN 2. *Ergreift das Gewehr!* [*Weapons at the ready!*]

HESSIANS. *Jawohl!*

JIM. *Wait!!*

HESSIAN 2. *Legt an!* [*Aim!*]

HESSIANS. *Jawohl!*

JIM. *Stop!!!*

    SMITH *raises his hand. Drum roll stops.*

SMITH. But as you will note from your souvenir programmes, this is only the first of *two* volumes, and you may now fortify yourselves before we continue. Refreshments may be found in the exterior and tobacco is to be enjoyed *outside* of the premises.

    Blackout.

    End of Act One.

ACT TWO

*A trumpet fanfare – perhaps a trio of alphorns. As lights rise we
face a row of conference chairs with low tables between. We are
now in the present. The general look is glossy and technologically
sophisticated. Seven panelists are seated, left to right:* BELINDA,
DICK, NTOMBI, PANDIT, IVAN, MARTIN, *and finally* ED. *In
front of each is a microphone and a placard displaying last
names. The men are dressed in dark suits – though some forgo ties
– and business attire for the women as well.*

BELINDA (*to us, posh, English*). Lovely. And welcome back to
all. And I hope we're all suitably refreshed. *But*: as I see from
the clock it is *just* gone five past so I'd like to get underway as
quickly as we can – And just to be clear: this is *not* the plenary
session. Plenary session is at *three*-thirty in the Zermatt Room,
and that's now been corrected online, so *do* be sure to check
the website because that information will always be the most
up to date. (*To the rear of the auditorium.*) And I trust we can
all hear in the back, yes? Brilliant. And I know there may be
latecomers what with the ice and snow and the security and
that's why I always recommend, whenever possible, *do* try to
take your lunch here in the conference centre, that way you'll
be sure to arrive back in plenty of time – (*To the panel.*)
Speaking of, did anyone have the *halibut*?

ED (*English, aristocratic*). I did, yes.

BELINDA. Nice, wasn't it?

ED. *Very* nice.

DICK. I had the beef.

PANDIT (*Indian accent*). I am vegetarian.

BELINDA. So kudos to the chef. And: for those *not* here this
morning, I'll just quickly *re*introduce – not that they *need*
introduction – going left to right, Sir Edward Branch, former
Chairman, BCHS Financial, London.

ED. Ed, please.

BELINDA. Martin Joosten, Executive Director, AmTek Energy Systems, Rotterdam.

MARTIN *nods politely.*

Ivan Peyankov, Distinguished Chair of the Lack Institute for Economic Research at the University of Chicago.

IVAN *nods.*

Pandit Pancholy, Chairman of UniPro Pacific, and a first-timer to this panel, I believe?

PANDIT. Hopefully not the last.

BELINDA. Ntombi Nkosi, Director of the Southern Africa Growth Alliance, or SAGA – and I know Ntombi has a flight at five-thirty so I've promised her we shan't run over.

NTOMBI *smiles.*

And as always, Richard Trumpett of TrumpettBank Global, LLC.

DICK (*bumptious, American – think Mitt Romney*). Good to be back.

BELINDA. And I'm Belinda Tate, of the Tate Foundation – oh, and *do* please turn off your phones if you haven't done so already. Or at least on silent. So: without *further* ado, I'd like to open it up as promised before lunch for a *quick* Q&A and hopefully we'll have Ntombi out no later than half-past.

NTOMBI (*joking, to* BELINDA, *English-African accent*). I need my frequent-flyer miles!

BELINDA (*with a sly laugh*). Of course you do. And I see some of us have already found our way to the microphones, so if we could keep it to one question apiece and then *do* try and step away so the next can have their turn, all right? And let's start right here in the back, shall we? Hello.

She indicates the back of the house, somewhere behind us we can't see. We hear a disembodied male voice, amplified.

MALE 1. Hello.

BELINDA. Hello.

MALE 1. And thank you for taking my question. Um. First, I wonder if the members of the panel would agree that the immediate crisis is now past for the Eurozone in the short term, and secondly, *if* so, whether we might expect markets to respond with greater confidence in the upcoming quarter?

BELINDA. Mm. Complex. Martin:

MARTIN (*Dutch-inflected perfect English*). Well, you know, it *is* a complex question and we should first acknowledge that we *are* still confronting dangerous levels of sovereign debt, primarily in Greece and Spain, and the effect of those risks, combined with the rise in commodity prices continues to create a great deal of market volatility –

BELINDA. Worrisome, yes.

MARTIN. – that being *said*, I *do* think that, on balance, the *immediate* outlook is actually surprisingly *positive* –

BELINDA (*pleasantly surprised*). Do you?

MARTIN (*with a laugh*). – I mean, if you'd said to me five years ago, if you'd said, come 2013 we'd be looking at revenues comparable to where they were pre-Lehman Brothers, I think most of us would've laughed in your face, but here we are in *precisely that situation*, so in point of fact, I think we should be feeling rather confident –

DICK. Absolutely.

MARTIN. – because among other things, there's been enormous opportunities for positive restructuring – (*Continues.*)

During MARTIN's *last line his microphone has begun to make an unpleasant noise.*

BELINDA (*overlapping*). Martin?

MARTIN. – and what *I've* seen in the aftermath has been streamlining and greater efficiency – (*Continues.*)

BELINDA (*overlapping*). Martin?

MARTIN. – which have contributed to a much more rapid recovery than any of us – (*Continues.*)

BELINDA (*overlapping*). Sorry –

MARTIN. – initially – is there some sort of – ?

BELINDA. I think we might be getting a *bit* of feedback from –

MARTIN. Is it me?

BELINDA (*to an* ATTENDANT). – Could we possibly get someone to – ?

DICK (*taking over, to* MALE 1). See, the beauty of the market is – it's a self-correcting system –

BELINDA. Dick:

An ATTENDANT *in slacks and pseudo-Tyrolean costume enters to adjust* MARTIN's *microphone*.

DICK. – left to its own devices. And the *real* threat to recovery, frankly, is not from deficits, per se, but from fear and overcorrection.

BELINDA (*to another unseen questioner*). Just here, then? To the other side?

A second MALE *voice, amplified*.

MALE 2. Um – yes –

BELINDA. Hello.

MALE 2. – um, I wonder if the panel could address the continuing loss of Western jobs to developing nations and also the labour conditions workers face in some of those places, and how those factors might be addressed as we move through the coming decade?

BELINDA. Mmm. Worrisome. Ivan?

IVAN. Yes. Well, you know, the problem with the question is, it presupposes that geographical boundaries present an obstacle to growth, which, strictly speaking, has not been the case for more than twenty years –

The ATTENDANT, *having finished, exits again*.

BELINDA (*quietly, to* MARTIN). Sorted out?

IVAN. – as historical nation-states are replaced by interdependent economies –

DICK. – In a global market –

IVAN. – in which regional dislocations are offset by broader market performance.

DICK. Put it this way: let's say a company in Cleveland decides it's in their interest to relocate production to Kowloon –

NTOMBI. Or Cameroon.

PANDIT. Or Chennai.

DICK. Now, is that *bad*?

PANDIT. Bad for *whom*?

DICK. Cuz when people say to *me* don'tcha care about *American* workers I say hey, ya know what? I care about people *all over the world*.

BELINDA. Pandit:

PANDIT. And of course the situation is the opposite from *our* point of view because the problem *we* face is not *un*employment but rather *underemployment* and how to best educate and integrate individuals into an expanding workforce.

BELINDA. Despite persistent poverty –

PANDIT (*dismissive*). Yes yes.

BELINDA. Median incomes some of the lowest in the world – ?

PANDIT. But this is not outsourcing, from *our* perspective, you see? It is *in*-sourcing. It is allowing innovation and competition to function exactly as Adam Smith intended.

DICK (*to* BELINDA). If I can jump in here?

BELINDA. I see Ntombi's hand –

DICK. I will defer –

BELINDA. Ntombi:

DICK. – to the lovely lady.

NTOMBI. Firstly, I would caution the questioner not to impose his own system of values, because *when* jobs like these come to emerging markets such as China, West Africa –

PANDIT. – Southern Asia.

NTOMBI. – where previously there were *none*, we are seeing *tangible difference* in the lives of poor people who now find access to a better way of life.

DICK. No question.

NTOMBI. And if the *nature* of these jobs – in mining, for example, or manufacturing – if they are distasteful to sensibilities in the West –

DICK. *Sensitivities*.

NTOMBI. Or if they are paid wages that might appear insufficient by Western standards, is that *exploitation*?

PANDIT. Or *opportunity*?

NTOMBI. Is it *slave labour*?

DICK. No one's *forcing* people to work.

NTOMBI. Or is it a matter that individual workers must decide for themselves?

BELINDA (*to us*). And of course *Africa* is of *primary* importance to the Tate Foundation and our commitment to ending modern-day slavery in the sub-Saharan region – (*Continues.*)

Other PANELISTS *murmur approvingly.*

BELINDA. – by coordinating between NGOs and local government.	DICK. Good for you.	NTOMBI. Yes, but that is a separate issue.
PANDIT. Yes, as we must.	IVAN. Very important.	MARTIN. Of course, and that's entirely commendable – (*Continues.*)

MARTIN. – but I think *Ntombi's* point – if I may – is that we must always be mindful to allow *local* economies to determine their own best response to international – (*Feedback squeals again.*) is it *me*?

BELINDA. Mmmnnno, still having a problem –

MARTIN. Is it something *I'm* doing?

IVAN. You can't touch it.

MARTIN. Who?

IVAN. You were touching it.

MARTIN. I wasn't touching it.

   ATTENDANT *returns to* MARTIN*'s side*.

DICK. Quick story?

BELINDA. Dick.

DICK. I was invited, coupla weeks ago, Congressman from my
   district said to me, said Dick, I want you to come talk to some
   kids – inner-city kids, ya know, underprivileged kids who don't
   have a whole lot of opportunities and I went to talk to these
   kids and one of 'em raises her hand – cute little kid – and she
   says to me, sir? Says, how can I make the world a better place?
   And I said well, lemme tell you what. I think that's a great
   goal, but if you really want to make the *world* a better place,
   first thing is you gotta do is *help yourself*.

   The ATTENDANT *finishes with* MARTIN*'s mic*.

BELINDA (*to* MARTIN). How're we doing?

MARTIN. Fingers crossed.

DICK. Cuz ya know, those of us in the financial sector – we get
   kind of a bad rap, ya know. People like to say there's been a
   culture of, I don't know, greed or self-interest, but my point to
   these kids was how does any of us expect to make a difference
   if you don't first *put yourself* in an economic position to do so?

BELINDA. We've got lots of hands. So first, the gentleman here,
   then the other side. Yes.

   Another unseen amplified MALE VOICE.

MALE 3. Hello.

BELINDA. Hello.

MALE 3. And thank you.

BELINDA. Thank *you*.

MALE 3. Yes, I was hoping to ask the panel, um, given, what we've seen in the past eighteen months, politically speaking? I mean, with some of the street protests – (*Continues*.)

BELINDA (*overlapping*). Yes. Mm.

MALE 3. – we've seen in response to the global recession and the perceived mismanagement of financial institutions and lack of corporate responsibility – (*Continues*.)

BELINDA (*overlapping*). Troubling.

MALE 3. – I wonder whether the panel feels we've arrived at any sort of turning point?

Slight pause. BELINDA *turns to* ED.

BELINDA. Well, if I might, I'd like to –

DICK. Sorry, you're talking about these people out there with all the *signs* and – ? (*Continues*.)

NTOMBI (*overlapping*). Well, a sense of frustration is understandable –

DICK. – and – and – and the *sleeping bags*?

NTOMBI. – but for the most part we're talking about a small number of disgruntled young people hoping to air their grievances in front of a sympathetic audience.

BELINDA. Actually –

PANDIT (*happily boastful*). You know, when people say to me Pandit, you know, you are part of *the one per cent*, I say to them, oh no! I am the *point zero zero one* per cent!

DICK (*to the questioner*). Problem is, there's a lot of misinformation out there –

BELINDA. But actually –

DICK. – and we need to do a better job communicating with these people and educating them about a system that actually works in their *favour*.

BELINDA. Actually, I'd like to ask Sir Edward, if I might?

ED. Hm?

BELINDA (*to* ED). Because I think your position is somewhat unique for this panel –

ED. Is it?

BELINDA. – having been at the centre of things for so long, and having now *removed* yourself –

ED. Retired, yes.

BELINDA. – it does lead me to wonder if your take is somewhat different?

ED (*carefully*). Well, erm, you know, I – I – I – *as* I sit here listening, I *do* start to wonder – the question occurs whether the past five years have taught us anything at all –

BELINDA. Does it?

ED. – I mean, there we were on the brink of utter disaster and yet here we sit, you know, five years on, trotting out some of the same bad ideas that caused all of our troubles to begin with –

BELINDA. Such as?

ED. – such as the mad rush to return to the excesses of five years ago, when we allowed the financial industry to overwhelm the productive economy to such a dangerous extent –

BELINDA. Yes.

ED. – and I do wonder whether the moment may have arrived to return to some limited form of regulation – (*Continues.*)

DICK (*overlapping, with a laugh*). Whoa, whoa, whoa, whoa –

ED. – to discourage markets from following their own mad impulses to the brink of catastrophe.

DICK. Well, you *could* do that. You could turn back the regulatory clock all the way to the nineteen-*seventies*, for that matter – (*Continues.*)

ED (*politely overlapping*). But that's not what I said.

DICK. – where you had an anti-dynamic economy in the UK, if you'll recall, which meant sluggish growth, massive unemployment – (*Continues*.)

| BELINDA (*to* DICK). I want give Sir Edward the chance to respond. | DICK. – an *enormous* credit contraction – (*To* BELINDA.) Sorry. | IVAN. Double-digit inflation. | ED. I'm not sure you heard me correctly. |

BELINDA. Sir Edward:

ED. I'm saying we've crashed the car *once*; do we really want to hand the keys back to the same drunken driver?

DICK. And you'd put the car in *neutral*.

BELINDA. Well, room for disagreement.

IVAN (*seconding* DICK). And historically, you know, these sorts of protests typically arise in response to cyclical downturns –

DICK (*with a shrug*). Cycle of *history*.

IVAN. – and then dissipate again upon recovery.

DICK. Sorry. *Speaking* of which –

BELINDA. Oh! *Nearly* forgot –

DICK. Shameless plug:

BELINDA. Dick has a *book*.

DICK. Hot off the press.

BELINDA. And tell us the title?

BELINDA *holds up a book with* DICK*'s glossy photo on the jacket.*

DICK. Called *The High Road*.

BELINDA (*reading from her notes*). *The High Road: Trumpetts of the New World*.

DICK. It's on Amazon.

BELINDA. And there you are on the jacket.

DICK. Big as life.

BELINDA. And it's more a *biography*, yes?

DICK. Quick story:

BELINDA. If it's quick.

DICK. Cuz if you trace the Trumpetts back to the eighteenth century – when you stop and think what life must've been like for those early Americans – kinda hardships they faced – cuz all they asked was the freedom to make a living – and that economic *freedom* is the one American export I think we can all agree on. That and Starbucks. (*Laughs at his own joke.*)

BELINDA (*to* MALE 3). Not really sure we answered your question, but –

DICK (*to* BELINDA). *What* was the question?

BELINDA. – anyway. Yes. The young woman toward the back?

We hear a FEMALE *voice – American accent.*

FEMALE. Hi.

BELINDA. Hello.

FEMALE. Um, I just had a quick question.

BELINDA. Perfect.

FEMALE. Yeah, um. I was just wondering how many houses you have?

Pause. The PANELISTS *stare, squint, squirm.*

IVAN (*off-mic, to* BELINDA). What is she asking?

BELINDA. Sorry, I'm not sure we correctly – ?

MARTIN (*to* BELINDA). *Houses*, she said?

IVAN (*to* FEMALE). *Whose* houses?

NTOMBI (*shielding her eyes, to* FEMALE). Who are you asking, darling?

FEMALE. The members of the panel?

BELINDA. How many *houses*?

MARTIN (*to* FEMALE). As in *homes*?

BELINDA (*to* FEMALE). As in *residences*?

FEMALE. Exactly.

The PANELISTS *exchange confused looks.*

BELINDA. Well, I – I – I – I don't want to speak for the members of –

PANDIT (*proudly unashamed*). Well, *I* can answer –

NTOMBI (*to* FEMALE). And why does that interest you?

PANDIT. I have *seven* houses. Three for my children, two for myself –

BELINDA (*to* FEMALE). Sorry, you don't mean his *personal* – ?

FEMALE. I do, yes.

PANDIT. – As well as two vacation homes.

BELINDA (*to* FEMALE). All right, then?

PANDIT. And two airplanes.

BELINDA. Grand.

FEMALE. Thank you.

BELINDA. Thank *you*. (*Longish beat, throat clear.*) So. Just here, then? I see another –

DICK (*interrupting* BELINDA, *irritated*). Sorry – do ya mind? Where's the person asked that?

BELINDA. Did she leave?

DICK (*shielding his eyes*). Where'd she go?

FEMALE (*on microphone*). I'm here.

BELINDA. There she is.

DICK. How ya doin'? (*With a chuckle.*) Uhhhh… Mind if I ask your name?

FEMALE (*beat*). I'd actually prefer not to say.

DICK (*with a laugh*). Uhhh… well, you just asked *us* a personal question –

BELINDA (*to* FEMALE). There *is* an open forum on housing at three o'clock –

DICK (*to* BELINDA). 'Scuse me. (*To* FEMALE.) So how 'bout if we were to ask *you* then, how many houses *you* have?

FEMALE. I live in an apartment.

DICK. Okay.

Pause. All stare.

IVAN (*privately, to* BELINDA). I have no idea what she's asking.

ED (*clears throat*). Well, *perhaps* what she's asking is whether it's time we began a more substantive conversation about capitalism, broadly speaking – (*Continues.*)

DICK (*overlapping*). No no no no. That wasn't the question.

ED. – because *some* have begun to question whether capitalism in its current form remains morally persuasive – (*Continues.*)

BELINDA. Yes. And we'll each have the opportunity to respond, so if we could – ?	DICK (*to* ED). Wait a second. She asked how many *houses* you have.	NTOMBI. No, the purpose of the question was to shame us. And I would like to say one thing to this woman:
PANDIT (*with a laugh*). Who is questioning this? *I* am not questioning!	MARTIN. But let's not go off on some meta-physical tangent.	ED. – or whether its philosophical underpinnings have been eroded by years of mistrust?

BELINDA. Ntombi:

NTOMBI (*to* FEMALE). I am not *ashamed* of having a nice house. I am not ashamed of having *several* houses. That is because I have a job and I *worked* for them.

ED. But for the past twenty-five years we've systematically
    stripped nearly *all* regulation from financial markets –
    (*Continues.*)

MARTIN. Creating the fastest   ED. – and in so doing, very
    growth in a hundred years.   nearly destroyed the world's
                                      economy – (*Continues.*)

ED. – in an attempt to enrich a tiny and privileged minority.

BELINDA (*seeing* PANDIT*'s raised hand*). Pandit:

PANDIT (*taking over, trying to end it*). I would like to say
    something to this young woman: my dear: there are many,
    many, poor people in the world. (*Continues.*)

BELINDA.   DICK (*snorts,*   NTOMBI. And   PANDIT. –
    And what,   *re:*   fewer every   There have
    then, is the   FEMALE).   day.   *always been*
    proper   Betcha she's   poor
    response?   not *poor*.   people –
                                                           (*Continues.*)

IVAN. In monkeys,   MARTIN. As was   ED. And they
    you know? In   ever the case.   *outnumber you.*
    clinical – In
    clinical –

PANDIT (*with a dismissive shrug*). There will *always be* poor
    people. But what *can we do* for these people – (*Continues.*)

BELINDA.   DICK. Exactly.   NTOMBI.   PANDIT. – if
    But, should   Create *jobs*.   they refuse
    government   Create   to help
    not bear   *incentives*.   themselves?
    some
    responsi-
    bility?
    (*Continues.*)

IVAN. If you look at   MARTIN. It is   ED. You can start by
    studies involving   perfectly clear   not *worsening*
    non-human   what we can do.   their lot.
    subjects –

BELINDA. Ivan:

IVAN. In rhesus monkeys, you know –

BELINDA (*to* IVAN). Say again?

IVAN. Rhesus monkeys.

BELINDA. Reese's – ?

DICK (*to* BELINDA). Monkeys.

BELINDA. Oh, *monkeys*.

IVAN. In clinical studies –

BELINDA. Thought he said *mongeese*.

IVAN. If one monkey pushes a lever and receives a cookie, and if the monkey in the next cage has to push the same lever one *hundred times* for the *same* cookie – (*Continues*.)

| BELINDA. Well, you'd have an angry monkey. | DICK (*laughing*). Better move to the other cage! | NTOMBI. *I'm sorry, but what does any of this mean?* |

| PANDIT. But monkeys are very, very nasty. | IVAN. – and if he notices the advantage the *first* monkey has – (*Continues*.) |

IVAN (*to* NTOMBI). – it means all primates have an instinctive conception of fairness.

DICK. Well, ya know what? Life's *not* fair. (*With a shrug*.) *Sorry*.

ED (*to* DICK). But why *legislate* unfairness? Wouldn't it seem redundant?

BELINDA. Moving on:

DICK (*to* ED). So how ya gonna make life fair, Ed? By taking from *me* and giving to *you*?

| DICK. Cuz, that's called *socialism*. – (*Continues*.) | PANDIT (*laughing*). Please, please! Don't take *my* money. | ED. Yes, it's known as *taxation*. |

DICK. – And what's unfair to *me*, ya see, is a system where the people who work hard, wind up giving all their money to support a buncha *freeloaders*.

MARTIN. And *if* the *goal* is to lift as many people out of poverty as possible, as I think we'd all agree, then there is one proven model for *achieving* that and that model is the free and unregulated international – (*Feedback again.*) *Oh for God's sake.*

  MARTIN *stands to exit.*

| BELINDA (*brightly*). Ah yes. And on *that* note, perhaps it might be best to bring this session to a close? | DICK (*to us*). Ya see, in this world ya got the *makers*, and then ya got the *takers*. And I know which side I'd rather be on. | NTOMBI (*to BELINDA*). We cannot lift the world if the world does not partic-pate in the lifting. | PANDIT (*to FEMALE*). I was born in a village with no running water. My father was a blacksmith. My mother was a seamstress. |

| MARTIN (*in disgust*). No. No. I'm sorry. This is simply ridiculous and symptomatic of a general level incompetence. | IVAN (*to DICK*). The results of this study have been replicated in dogs, in birds, but never in human beings. | ED (*to DICK*). And when you divide the world into two adversarial camps, Dick, what do you imagine is the likely outcome? |

  MARTIN *exits in a huff as the* FEMALE *makes her way to the front of the stage, dressed like a student, with knapsack.*

BELINDA. And I'd like to thank the members of the panel –

DICK (*re:* FEMALE). Is that her? Is that the one?

BELINDA (*to us*). And I'd especially thank all of *you* –

DICK (*to* FEMALE). Lemme explain something: the *world*, ya see, the world is not a *charity* with *you* as the sole beneficiary. (*Continues.*)

BELINDA. And one *quick* reminder about the – Ah. It would seem I've rather lost control, wouldn't it?

DICK. Hate to break it to ya. And maybe if ya'd tried *working* for a living you might've figured that out by now – (*Continues.*)

NTOMBI (*to* FEMALE). Get yourself a *job*, darling. Go and find a nice, steady *job*, all right?

PANDIT (*to* FEMALE). But *I* dreamed of some day having a great deal of money, you see, and now I have it!

IVAN. And these results have been replicated in chimpanzees, in dogs, even certain species of birds –

ED (*to* DICK). And *if* we continue on this same course we are sowing the seeds of our undoing.

DICK. – so let me give ya one little piece of advice:

The FEMALE *has taken out a compressed-air horn and now sounds a sustained blast. The* ATTENDANT *blows an extremely loud whistle. Sounds of doors opening – drums and chanting from outside.*

BELINDA (*to the* FEMALE). No no no no no. Oh dear. Sorry? I really must ask you to respect the rules of the conference. This is not in our charter.

DICK. *Oh, for fuck's sake.* Will somebody get these assholes out of here, please? Unbelievable. And where the hell's the goddamn *security*?

NTOMBI. How did they gain access to this room? Is there no one to take control of this? (*To* FEMALE.) *Behave yourselves! Behave yourselves!!*

PANDIT. Ladies and gentlemen, let us be civil. You only discredit yourselves by behaving in this way.

ED. There you are, Dick. Is this what you want? I ask you, is this a vision of the future that you would embrace? Then I leave you to it.

*An alarm begins to sound. From overhead a spray-painted
banner is unfurled reading: 'OVERTHROW FEP'. The*
ATTENDANT *pulls a balaclava over his head, produces a
manifesto, begins to read. More* PROTESTERS *swarm the
aisles and stage area. A smoke grenade is thrown onstage. The*
PANELISTS *rise and exit making phone calls as they go.*

ATTENDANT.
*Article One: We
call for the imme-
diate dissolution
of the FEP and its
governing body
and the renuncia-
tion of its current
policies by partic-
ipating member
states. Article
Two: Creation of
an international
citizens tribunal
to oversee and re-
strict governmen-
tal collusion with
private industry.
Article Three –*

FEMALE (*on bull-
horn*). Attention
FEP members:
this is an illegiti-
mate assembly
and does not rep-
resent the con-
cerns of working
people, women or
minorities, and
has as its sole
function the con-
tinued subversion
of workers' rights
by corporate prof-
iteering. Our
grievances
include the
following:

BELINDA. Erm – I
wonder, is there
an administrative
person who could
possibly step in,
here? Because
none of this was
contained in my
information
packet.

DICK (*on phone*).
Listen, do me a
favour. Tell 'em
to bring the car
around to the
back entrance. I
dunno, it's a total
shitstorm in here.
How the hell
should I know?
Some bullshit
with these ass-
holes –

NTOMBI (*to
FEMALE*). *You
are behaving like
animals. And
when you behave
like animals you
will be treated
like animals.* (*On
phone.*) Yes,
change of plans.
No, I am taking
the earlier flight.

PANDIT (*to us*).
Please, if what
you need are jobs,
there are many,
many to be had in
my country. It is a
beautiful country
and you are wel-
come to visit at
any time, but you
must behave
peacefully.
Namaste.

SECURITY POLICE *with helmets, truncheons and riot shields enter at a run.* PROTESTERS *bolt for the doors.* BELINDA *is last to exit.*

BELINDA (*to us, as she exits*). *And please check the website for further information!!*

The alarm continues as we stare at the empty stage, then abruptly cuts off. Long silence. After a bit, SMITH *awkwardly emerges out of the smoke and chaos, surveying the damage. He looks at us, smiles sheepishly.*

SMITH. I do apologise.

He opens his folio, finds his place, clears throat.

Chapter Three.

Drum roll resumes. The conference chairs and the wall behind it go away and we pick up where we left off at the end of Act One: the blindfolded JIM *against the wall facing the firing squad.*

HESSIAN 2 (*sabre aloft*). *Kraft des mir von Seiner Majestät George dem Dritten verliehenen Rechts erkläre ich diesen Mann zu einem Feind der Krone, der sein Leben verwirkt hat. Alle dafür?* [*By the power vested in me by His Majesty George III, I hereby pronounce this man an enemy of the Crown and in forfeit of his life. All in favour?*]

HESSIANS. *Jawohl!*

JIM. *But you've not the authority!!*

HESSIAN 2. *Ergreift das Gewehr!* [*Weapons at the ready!*]

HESSIANS. *Jawohl!*

JIM. *Wait!!*

HESSIAN 2. *Legt an!* [*Aim!*]

HESSIANS. *Jawohl!*

JIM. *Stop!!!*

The tavern door abruptly opens and COLONEL – *formerly Captain* – SHIRLEY *from Act One appears, napkin in his collar, glass of sherry, playing cards.*

SHIRLEY (*brisk, as always*). I say, Lieutenant?

HESSIAN 2 (*to the* HESSIANS). *Halt!*

   HESSIAN 2 *salutes* SHIRLEY. *Drum roll stops.*

SHIRLEY. *Bit* of a racket, wouldn't you say?

HESSIAN 2. Jawohl, Kommandeur.

SHIRLEY. Game of cards here, you know?

HESSIAN 2. Es tut mir leid, zir!

SHIRLEY. *Do* try to keep it down, won't you? Thanks much.

JIM. *Can ya do nothing to help me, sir!!!?*

SHIRLEY. What's that?

JIM. *Can ya not put a stop to this gross miscarriage of justice?*

SHIRLEY. Erm – Well, it would appear you're to be executed, wouldn't it?

JIM. *But whatever for?*

SHIRLEY. Lieutenant?

HESSIAN 2. Jawohl?

SHIRLEY. Why is it we're executing this fellow?

HESSIAN 2. Becoss he iss enemy of ze Crown!!

SHIRLEY. Is he? (*To* JIM.) Well – Out of my hands, I'm afraid.

JIM. *But why am I an enemy?*

SHIRLEY (*to* HESSIAN 2). Why is he an enemy?

HESSIAN 2. Becoss he vill not pay tax!

SHIRLEY (*small laugh, to* JIM). Well, we've all got to pay our taxes, don't we? (*To* HESSIAN 2.) Carry on.

HESSIAN 2. And becoss he is zon of Vashington. (*Raising his sabre.*) *Ergreift das Gewehr!*

   Drum roll resumes. SHIRLEY *stops, thinks.*

HESSIANS. *Jawohl!!*

SHIRLEY. Hang on. Hang on. Sorry.

HESSIAN 2 (*finger to his lips, to the* DRUMMER). *Leise!*

The drum roll drops to half-volume.

SHIRLEY (*to* HESSIAN). No no no – *Stop*.

HESSIAN (*to* HESSIANS). *Halt!!*

Drum roll stops.

SHIRLEY. Sorry – You did say *Washington*?

HESSIAN George Vashington, jawohl, Kommandeur.

SHIRLEY (*to* JIM). You there, with the blindfold? Is this true?

JIM. I – I – I know not how best to answer ya, sir –

SHIRLEY. No no. *Are* you telling us, then, that your father is Commander-in-Chief of the Colonial Revolutionary Forces?

JIM. Not if it displease His Majesty!

SHIRLEY (*impatient*). Yes, understood, I'm only asking whether you are, factually speaking, his legitimate offspring?

JIM (*beat*). I'm but a poor bastard that's travelling this road to Virginia to find the man what never have the heart to call me his own.

HESSIAN 2 (*to* SHIRLEY). Is zon of Vashington, ja?

SHIRLEY (*dubious*). So 'twould *seem*.

HESSIAN 2 *raises his sabre. Drum roll.*

HESSIAN 2. *Ergreift das Gewe– !!* [*Weapons at the re–*]

SHIRLEY (*frustrated*). No, no, no, no. *Stop!!*

HESSIAN 2. *Halt!!!*

Drum roll stops.

SHIRLEY. For heaven's sake, Lieutenant. Don't *kill* him.

HESSIAN 2. Jawohl.

SHIRLEY. Take him *hostage*.

JIM. Oh, bless ya, sir! Bless ya fer that!

HESSIAN 2 (*to* SHIRLEY). Hasstache?

SHIRLEY. Hostage? (*Trying to explain with gestures*.) I. Want *you* – Oh, *barnacles*.

JIM (*to* SHIRLEY). Yer a true gentleman, sir, and a credit to yer regiment.

SHIRLEY *pulls a phrase book from his pocket*.

SHIRLEY (*searching for translation*). Hang on. Hang on. Erm – Nehmen sie – ?

HESSIAN 3. Nehmen?

HESSIAN 2 (*pointing to the tavern*). Mit ins *Haus* nehmen? [Take him *inside*?]

SHIRLEY. No no.

HESSIAN 2 (*pointing to* JIM). Err… *Hops* nehmen? [Arrest him?]

SHIRLEY. Ah. Here we are – *Geisel*?

HESSIAN 2. Ahh!! Sie meinen *Geisel*? [Ahh, you meant – *hostage*?]

SHIRLEY. Exactly.

HESSIAN 2 (*with a laugh*). Das hatte ich nicht verstanden! [I didn't understand you!]

SHIRLEY. Quite.

HESSIAN 2 (*to* HESSIANS). *Nehmt ihn als Geisel!* [*Take him hostage!!*]

The HESSIANS *untie* JIM *as a genteel, well-dressed man –* ISAAC LOW *– appears at the door.*

LOW (*cultivated, highbrow, to* SHIRLEY). Are we done with wagering?

SHIRLEY. *I'm* ripe for sport.

LOW. Yes – I'm a *trifle* weary –

SHIRLEY. Another hand?

LOW. – and the hour *does* grow late.

SHIRLEY. Admitting defeat, are you?

LOW. Travelling at sunrise, you know?

SHIRLEY. As you will.

LOW (*consulting his paper*). Tabulating your winnings here.
'Twould seem you've rather soundly vanquished me.

SHIRLEY. Well, luck played a part.

LOW (*using glasses*). Let's see: twenty-seven hands at whist, of
which you took twenty-three, at twelve shillings a hand –
Erm… twenty-three times twelve, subtracting your four–

JIM (*still blindfolded*). Fifty-seven guineas, sir.

LOW (*beat*). Say again?

JIM. Or two hundred twenty-eight shillings. Or nineteen pounds,
five pence, in common value. And I can gladly calculate the
rate of exchange in both pieces of eight and Continental notes,
if that be yer currency.

LOW. Who is this?

SHIRLEY. Prisoner, you know.

LOW. On what charge?

SHIRLEY. Wouldn't pay his taxes.

LOW (*with a laugh*). Ah, *well*. (*To* JIM.) What *you* lack, my boy,
is an *accountant*.

SHIRLEY *and* LOW *start to exit as* BLANKE *and*
CONSTANCE *enter at a run, lanterns in hand.*

CONSTANCE (*out of breath, re:* JIM). *Good sirs, I do beseech
you hold a moment and surrender this man.*

SHIRLEY. Gently. *Gently.*

CONSTANCE. My name is Constance Pugh, and I do accuse this
fellow of a most vile misdeed upon my person.

SHIRLEY. Oh *dear.*

CONSTANCE. As I lay sleeping this night he did enter my
bedchamber and lay athwart me while stifling my mouth and
holding the point of a kitchen knife to my throat –

A HESSIAN *pulls a knife from* JIM*'s belt.*

– the very same, aye, and did avail himself of me most brazenly, for which I can offer indisputable proof, for he does bear the mark of a halfpenny coin upon his hindmost parts.

BLANKE. Which I may corroborate –

CONSTANCE. Whereafter he did open our vestry and appropriate to himself the sacramental items we do employ upon the Sabbath –

Another HESSIAN *removes a wooden altarpiece from* JIM's *bag.*

– no doubt to sell them for coins to line his pocket and I would have the full measure of the law now brought against him for his manifold crimes.

LOW *signals to remove* JIM's *blindfold.*

LOW (*to* JIM). Erm. Know you this intemperate young lady?

JIM. She is a stranger to *me*, sir – (*Continues.*)

JIM. – and clearly suffers from some form of mental derangement.	CONSTANCE (*to* JIM, *before being silenced*). *I shall cut out your tongue by the very root if you dare to lie again.*	SHIRLEY (*calmly to* HESSIANS, *re:* CONSTANCE). Take hold of her. Restrain her, please.

BLANKE. How can you stand upon solid ground and profess such outright lies?	LOW. For I'll admit I'm a trifle bewildered.

Two HESSIANS *restrain* CONSTANCE *and stifle her mouth.*

BLANKE (*to* LOW). This lady is a virtuous soul who did offer this fellow naught but charity.

SHIRLEY (*to* CONSTANCE). And the Negro is?

BLANKE. My name is John Blanke, sir –

JIM (*to* LOW, *re:* BLANKE). The Negro is *mine*, as attested to by the bill of sale you'll find in this pocket, dated not twenty-four hours past –

LOW *pulls the contract from* JIM*'s pocket.*

– in which time he's both held me at gunpoint, and defied my ev'ry command and if there's any should be in custody 'tis surely *he*.

LOW (*inspecting the contract*). You say your name is *Blanke*?

BLANKE. Indeed 'tis, and yet –

LOW. And yours, *Trumpett*, I take it?

JIM. The same.

LOW (*to* BLANKE). Well, it does herein stipulate you *are* this fellow's property – (*Continues*.)

BLANKE (*overlapping*). Which I do dispute.

LOW. – which you are free to contest but this document would seem to militate against you.

BLANKE. I am the rightful Earl of Rivington, sir, and none may lay claim to me.

JIM. The devil would say aught to gain your favour – (*Continues*)

BLANKE (*overlapping*). Bring forth a Bible and I shall swear it.

JIM (*re:* CONSTANCE). – and *this* one's motive I cannot hazard, 'less she did espy me bathing and concocted these fantasies out of carnal frustration –

Somehow CONSTANCE *manages to take hold of the sabre from the* HESSIAN *that holds her. She places it at* JIM*'s chest as the* HESSIANS *train their muskets on her.*

LOW. Carefully! Carefully!	HESSIAN 2 (*to* HESSIANS). *Ergreift das Ge-wehr!!!* [*Weapons at the ready!!*]	CONSTANCE. *Release him to me or his blood shall moisten this ground!*

SHIRLEY. Oh, *really*. I hardly see the need for the histrionics – (*Continues*.)	JIM. Look, sir! She's plainly in the throes of an erotic frenzy!

SHIRLEY (*to* CONSTANCE). – And I should inform you, these men are authorised to fire upon those offering lethal resistance, into which category you increasingly place yourself.

A stand-off. CONSTANCE *breathes hard.*

LOW (*to* BLANKE). Were any witness to the alleged misdeed upon this lady?

BLANKE. I… do confess, I was preoccupied with – with – with –

LOW. Then, none can verify the claim?

CONSTANCE. Is my solemn word so unreliable?

LOW (*a condescending chuckle*). My dear, I have a daughter of your years, and I daresay I'd neither call her solemn *or* reliable.

SHIRLEY (*chuckling*). Very good.

HESSIAN 2 (*quietly, to* SHIRLEY). Was hat er gesagt? [What did he say?]

SHIRLEY. Erm – *Frauleins*, you know?

The HESSIANS *all chuckle.*

HESSIANS. Ja. / Dumme schlampen. / Mecker liese. / Zickig. (*Etc.*)

CONSTANCE (*to* SHIRLEY). You mean to say, then, you will not prosecute my charge?

LOW. My dear girl –

CONSTANCE. If not for the assault then surely for the theft?

JIM (*to* CONSTANCE). Fer you'd know nothing of thievery, would ya? (*Continues.*)

CONSTANCE *pushes the sword into* JIM's *chest. The* HESSIANS *cock their weapons.*

| JIM. – And where's the coin purse ya did – *ahh! Protect me, sir!* | CONSTANCE (*to* JIM). *Do you feel this now, or shall I make it more sensible for you?* | BLANKE (*to* CONSTAN-CE). *Good lady! You cannot suc-ceed here!* (*Continues.*) | SHIRLEY(*to* HESSIA-NS). No no. Halt! Nicht – Oh bug-ger. Erm – *Nicht schießen!* |

BLANKE. – Temper your fury, I beg you, and let justice take its course.

CONSTANCE. There never was *justice* in this world, Mister Blanke. Were you never taught this? There was only ever *violence* and *gold*.

CONSTANCE *flings sabre to the ground, spits.*

(*Quietly to* JIM.) Damned be your soul, sir, and damned your fucking lies.

SHIRLEY (*prudishly*). Language!

CONSTANCE *exits into the darkness.*

HESSIAN 2 (*quietly, to* HESSIANS). Sie menstruiert, ja? [She's got her period, huh?]

The HESSIANS *laugh.*

LOW (*to* BLANKE). Erm – you did say *Rivington*?

BLANKE. Do you know it, sir?

LOW. You're not referring to the late Mister John Andrews?

BLANKE. I was his ward.

JIM. And I, the son of Mister George Washington!

Beat. Confused looks. SMITH *takes over as all parties continue the inaudible discussion.*

SMITH. And lest the untangling of this confusion prove tedious to the listener –

LOW (*quietly, to* SHIRLEY). Of *Virginia*?

SMITH. – we shall abbreviate the telling to say only that, within the space of several months, Mister Trumpett and his servingman were to find themselves in an altogether more pleasant prospect.

Music – a minuet or allemande. Title reads 'THE CITY OF NEW YORK'. Exit HESSIANS, BLANKE, SHIRLEY *and* JIM *as the space transforms. Chandeliers descend and* SERVANTS *in livery bring gilded chairs.* LOW *remains.*

Mister Isaac Low was a gentleman of some fortune in Venezuelan silver, who found himself at mid-life in position to encourage the prosperity of others through private equity and the sponsorship of industry. He served as delegate to the Continental Congress and President of the First Chamber of Commerce, where his prudence was as noteworthy as his generosity.

MARGARITA *enters, joining* LOW.

Mrs Low – called Margarita at home – was as prominent in *fashionable* society as Mister Low in the financial, and together they were celebrated for their liberality, their broad-minded outlook and philanthropic largesse.

She whispers in his ear, he in hers.

Their residence stood at the southern end of Manhattan Island near the corner of Gold Street and Maiden Lane, at which location are presently to be found both a branch office of J.P. Morgan Chase and Company, and a Kentucky Fried Chicken.

JIM *enters, met by a* FOOTMAN *who bows and relieves him of his hat and his bags.*

And though the house was modest by the standards of the gentry, Jim Trumpett had ne'er seen the like. And as he surveyed the setting into which he found himself newly thrust, he had the distinct sensation of having finally arrived at precisely where he had always belonged.

Music stops. JIM *takes it in.*

Chapter Four.

Lightning, thunder, darkness – not unlike the beginning of Act One, only this storm has the chintzy feeling of theatrical device. A makeshift stage appears, hung with draperies. BLANKE *walks into a spotlight, dressed in velvet, announcing grandly:*

BLANKE. The Extraordinary Narrative of My Origin and Singular Upbringing, by Mister John Blanke of Rivington, Lancashire, late of Dahomey. Part One: My Abduction.

The curtains part to reveal a poorly painted tropical scene. A harpsichord plays an arpeggio and a masque unfolds onstage as BLANKE *sings:*

Onye mere nwa nebe akwa.
Egbe mere nwa nebe akwa.
Weta uziza weta ose.
Weta ngaji nkuru ofe.
Umu nnunu aracha ya –

Onstage, an ACTOR *enters as* YOUNG BLANKE, *followed by two other* ACTORS *as bearded* PIRATES, *who approach him stealthily and capture him in a canvas bag.* YOUNG BLANKE *struggles within the bag as the* PIRATES *pantomime laughter and brandish wooden swords. One* PIRATE *inadvertently knocks over a bit of scenery.*

(*Losing his shit.*) Nay, nay, nay – *Stop! Stop, I say, and give me light!!*

LOW (*a voice in the darkness*). Daylight, please?

Music stops. Window shutters are thrown open, filling the room with sunlight. It becomes apparent that we have been watching a dress rehearsal. In front of the little stage sit LOW, MARGARITA *and their sixteen year-old daughter,* DELILAH.

SMITH. By late-midsummer Mister Trumpett and Mister Blanke had established themselves essential components of the Low household, with Mister Blanke – it must be said – their especial favourite.

MARGARITA (*to* BLANKE). Is aught amiss, John?

BLANKE. Is – ? *Why, 'tis plainly a travesty, ma'am!*

MARGARITA. O, say not so!	LOW. No no no, nothing of the sort!	DELILAH. However so? Not to *my* eye!

BLANKE (*berating the* ACTORS). I mean, have you no feeling for the gravity of – ? (*To* MARGARITA.) 'Tis a most monstrous human wickedness we would depict and here they've endowed it with all the solemnity of a minstrel burlesque!

MARGARITA. But 'twas *engrossing*.

BLANKE. 'Twas an *embarrassment*. (*Continues*.)

The ACTORS *remove their masks and beards.*

Further, all the accoutrements are shoddy and visibly threadbare –

DELILAH (*raising her hand*). Mister Blanke?

BLANKE. – and I'd sooner abandon the performance outright than provide low *comedy* where we should provoke *nobler* sentiments.

DELILAH. A question?

BLANKE. Lady?

DELILAH. Are there not *tigers* in the jungle?

LOW. Is it possible, John, you're being a *trifle* severe?

BLANKE. I have striven, sir, for *weeks*, with this the result, and the performance not two weeks from the day –

LOW. Well, have another go.

BLANKE. – no, I tell you, 'tis impossible. Forgive me. I do apologise but 'tis beyond my power to achieve.

BLANKE *exits dramatically, passing* JIM *who has entered at a discreet distance in business attire, with ledger, pen and inkwell.*

LOW. Ohhhh, *dear*. (*To* MARGARITA.) Follow him, Pearlie. You have his confidence.

MARGARITA. But might we not compound his anguish? I mean, he's frightfully *sensitive* –

LOW. No no no no no.

MARGARITA. – and perhaps it's asking too much, to make publick display of him –

LOW (*to* DELILAH). Go with your mother.

MARGARITA. – though, he is so artfully *eloquent* on the topic.

DELILAH. Come, Mama. Let us condole with him. [*NB:* DELILAH *says 'Mama' and 'Papa' with emphasis on the second syllable.*]

LOW. That's the stuff!

MARGARITA. But we'll approach him gingerly.

LOW. And fetch him back with you.

MARGARITA *and* DELILAH *exit, passing* JIM.

MARGARITA (*quietly chatting to* DELILAH, *as they go*). I mean, *I* found it rather *compelling*.

DELILAH (*likewise*). But shouldn't there be *tigers*?

LOW *waves away the* ACTORS, *who bow and exit as* JIM *steps forward*.

JIM. Sir?

LOW. Yes, Jim?

JIM (*offering ledger and pen*). Your signature?

SMITH. And if Mister Blanke found *sentimental* favour within the family, Mister Trumpett's contribution was somewhat more indispensible.

JIM. Just here.

LOW *dons glasses to sign. Exit* SMITH.

LOW (*with a sigh*). Poor Mister Blanke. I fear we've placed him in an untenable position –

JIM. And here again.

LOW. – and I claim no knowledge of the *performing* arts, mind you –

JIM. And your initials beneath.

LOW. – but he has the artistic *temperam*– What am I signing?

JIM (*all business*). A letter to Mister Cumpsty?

LOW. Cumpsty, yes?

JIM. Informing him that we find him in default and proposing a schedule of payment –

LOW (*as he signs*). Oh dear.

JIM. – such that, should we receive no instalment by Friday next we shall foreclose upon his granary.

LOW. Pity.

JIM (*next item*). A Mister Schuyler of Trenton writes to solicit your investment of some twenty-seven hundred pounds –

LOW. Preston Schuyler?

JIM. – for purposes of establishing a foundry –

LOW. Well, I think we may.

JIM (*dissuading him*). Iron manufacturey has shewn a seven per cent decline owing to wartime disruptions in pig iron, and I'd counsel 'gainst any venture that does not return at the highest neat revenue.

LOW. And this?

JIM. This does empower me to place the sum of seven thousand pounds in the account of Mister Lagarde in the Tortugas.

LOW. *Seven* – ?

JIM. Thousand.

LOW. Yet you deny Mister *Schuyler*?

JIM. Mister Schuyler requests an *advance*.

LOW. Whereas, Lagarde?

JIM. Will place his in *circulation*.

LOW (*beat*). Erm – ?

JIM. Mister Lagarde is owed some twenty thousand pounds in outstanding debt, a portion of which we hereby *purchase* from him at a reduced rate, collateralised against your fixed assets –

LOW (*trying to follow*). Purchase his *debts*.

JIM. – upon condition that, in borrowing from *you,* we do permit *him* leverage that same obligation against *his* creditors, so the risk now falls upon *them* –

LOW (*lost*). I – I – I –

JIM. – whereat, upon collection of the *original* debt, we do derive our percentage and the process begins anew.

LOW. And – and – and – you're quite sure none of this trespasses upon the strict boundary of… shall we say, *illegality*?

JIM. In what sense?

LOW. Well – whenever a transaction reaches a certain level of *complexity* –

JIM. This method is common practice in all European houses – (*Continues*.)

LOW (*overlapping*). No, no. I'm sure you're correct –

JIM. – and as your rate of charitable giving is ultimately unsustainable –

LOW. Is it?

JIM. – for if you do continue at present pace you will in time erode the advantage you enjoy over your competitors.

LOW. But – is it in the spirit of *charity*, Jim, to talk of *competition* – ?

JIM. You do compete for the good opinion of society, do you not? In which you are surely foremost?

LOW (*flattered*). I – I – well, *indeed*, but if we would intend the betterment of publick –

JIM (*theoretically*). If a man's fortune remains *constant*, sir, while that of his neighbour does *increase* then would not that man, over time, as a simple arithmetical truth, become a *pauper*, relative to his neighbour?

LOW (*mumbling, losing his way*). Hardly a *pauper*.

JIM. And any man that willingly makes of himself a pauper for *reputation's* sake I would take to be a *fool*, sir. Which, I daresay, you'd never be.

LOW. Well, that is why we hired *you*.

JIM (*seamlessly shifting topic*). As to domestic concerns?

LOW. Aye?

A SERVANT *brings a glass of sherry for* LOW.

JIM. Specifically, my lodgings?

LOW (*to* SERVANT). Thank you, Faraday.

JIM. Though I hesitate to mention it, but Mister *Blanke* has recently been given improved accommodations and I've taken note that his new chamber is nearly of equal dimension to my *own*.

LOW (*unmoved*).... Yes?

JIM. My *servant*, sir.

LOW. I – I – I – well, Mister Blanke is – is – is an *exceptional* –

JIM. But is it proper?

LOW. Well – admittedly –

JIM. I can shew you the measurements.

LOW (*giving in*). No, no. We – we – we shall... address the discrepancy.

JIM. Thank you, sir. And secondly – in the matter of your daughter?

LOW. Yes?

JIM. For, it cannot escape one's attention that, with a young woman such as Miss Low, accustomed as she is to certain indulgences –

LOW. Well, the ladies have their needs, you know?

JIM. But, as you do depend on her to ensure continuance of the fortune you've sought to accumulate – there is the matter of a suitable attachment?

LOW (*wary*).... Yes?

JIM. And it seems to me that if connexion were to be made within a fixt perimeter –

LOW (*warier still*).... Yes?

JIM. – for, at the conclusion of the present hostilities, as I would remind you, I *do* stand to receive a substantial sum from my paternal relations –

But before he can continue, BLANKE *is dragged back in by* MARGARITA *and* DELILAH.

MARGARITA. Look who we've brought you, Zacky!

LOW. *There's* the fellow! Bravo, John!

BLANKE. Nay, truly –

DELILAH. Bravissimo!!

BLANKE. – let us speak of it no further.

LOW. No no. As I was expressing to Mrs Low – for this is what we lack, you see? Why waste our time upon *superficial* entertainment when a work of *substance* such as yours can – can – can illuminate a *social ill* –

MARGARITA. – and so *movingly*!

BLANKE. But – not to overstate the – might it not be simpler to write a *letter*? Given your connexions?

LOW (*beat*). A letter to – ?

BLANKE. Could we not craft a petition in opposition to the practice, to which those in attendance could be signatory –

MARGARITA. But – but – but – but a *play*, John! *Think* of it – expresses so many things a petition cannot!

BLANKE. But what need we the *play*, if we might effect *legislation*?

MARGARITA. You *shed light* upon *injustice*.

BLANKE. And 'twill have the opposite effect if 'tis performed with ineptitude, and – (*Continues.*)

LOW (*overlapping*). 'Twill be ready on the night!

BLANKE. – and – and – and though I'd no more impose upon your generosity –

MARGARITA. Never hesitate!

BLANKE. – 'tis merely – these stage dressings were repurposed from a travelling carnival, and if we could only fashion *new* ones – ?

LOW. Jim?

JIM. Sir?

LOW. Could you withdraw another hundred pounds for Mister Blanke so that – (*To* BLANKE.) will a hundred be sufficient?

JIM. On what account, sir?

LOW. Oh, the household, I should think.

JIM. That is now under *my* direction, sir –

DELILAH (*irritated*). Oh, *pooh*.

JIM. – as you did authorise, and I'd not further deplete it.

LOW. Or, the equity fund, then?

JIM. Once again – (*Continues*.)

JIM. – those	LOW. But	DELILAH	MARGARITA
funds are	surely there	(*bored*).	*pretends to*
properly	are discre-	Hey-ho!	*doze off and*
sequestered	tionary –		*snore.*
– (*Con-*	Pardon us,		
tinues.)	ladies.		

JIM. – so as to remain distinct from your *charitable* giving –

MARGARITA (*breezily*). What have we given to this year, Zacky?

LOW. Erm – let's see – we financed the rebuilding of the almshouse?

MARGARITA. I'd nearly forgotten!

LOW. Forg– ? Why, your name is inscribed above the entryway in gilded letters!

DELILAH (*sitting in LOW's lap*). I want to have *my* name on something!

JIM. And, when you do squander those funds on African pantomimes –

DELILAH. Can't *I* do something for Africa, Papa?

LOW (*chucking her under the chin*). Aren't you *good*!

DELILAH. I'm going to put a score of my childhood dresses into a box and send them straight away to the little Hottentot girls!

LOW (*as an alternative*). Suppose you take up a *collection*, at the next cotillion, say, among all the young sparks and we'll put it on a boat bound for the Bight of Benin!

DELILAH. Could it have my *name* on it?

LOW. Why ever not?

DELILAH. For all to see?

LOW. We'll paint it right above the scupper, the *Good Ship Delilah Low*!

DELILAH. *Hurrah!*

LOW (*removing* DELILAH *from his lap*). Up you go, now. And Jim?

JIM. Sir?

   LOW *rises*. DELILAH *flounces out of the room*.

LOW. Do see to Mister Blanke's request.

BLANKE. Bless you, sir.

LOW. Now, tend to your master, John. (*To* JIM.) We shan't monopolise him further.

   LOW *and* MARGARITA *exit*.

JIM (*to* BLANKE, *as he writes*). I've requested a change of quarters, and Mister Low has agreed. You'll see my belongings are transferred where he should designate?

BLANKE. You take exception to your rooms?

JIM. You needn't trouble yerself – (*Continues*.)

BLANKE (*overlapping*). You were pleased enough before.

JIM. – with the reasoning, John, simply do as I ask.

BLANKE (*beat*). Aye.

JIM. And the carpets need a thorough beating. Also, my left riding boot has shed its heel and I'll want it replaced by Friday so if ya'd carry it to the cobbler's for me –

BLANKE. Are we to be travelling?

JIM. We are not.

BLANKE. Then, what is the urgency?

JIM (*beat*). I intend to take Miss Low for a canter 'round Delancey Square.

BLANKE (*beat, dubious*). And has Mister Low given consent?

JIM. Wherefore must ya quibble with me on ev'ry – ?

BLANKE. I only suggest your station might not recommend you for the privilege.

JIM. Do ya?

BLANKE. With respect.

JIM. Cuz *you've* no shortage of privileges, have ya?

BLANKE. If I do find favour –

JIM. And 'tis awful curious how I do labour late into the evening while my servingman perches atop the parlour cushions talking matters philosophical with them whose stables he oughta rightly be shovellin' the shit from.

BLANKE. Mister Low has a virtuous heart – (*Continues.*)

JIM (*overlapping, muttering*). I'm sure ya've had a good long look at it – (*Continues.*)

BLANKE (*overlapping*). – and I hold him in esteem.

JIM. – from the way ya keep yer head shoved up his ass all day – (*Without stopping, to* FARADAY.) – *What?*

FARADAY *waits at the door.*

FARADAY. Mister Lagarde.

JIM. Aye.

FARADAY *goes.*

BLANKE. And if you'd but consider my request Mister Low would readily buy out my contract – (*Continues.*)

JIM (*overlapping, calmly writing*). Well, I'm not in the market fer a *sale*, am I?

BLANKE. – and for the price you'd have three servingmen equal to myself.

JIM *ignores* BLANKE, *writes, as* SMITH *returns.*

I'm thirty-seven years of age, sir. The greater part of which I have spent in the service of –

JIM (*looking up*). O, fer the blood of – All I do ask is ya tidy my fuckin' room and post a parcel fer me once a week when ya're not too busy swanking about in yer velvety trousers – where d'ya think ya'll come by another master half as obligin' as me?

BLANKE. As 'I'.

JIM. Got yer own quarters, free and clear, and pampered like a fuckin' spaniel – *what more would you have of me*?

BLANKE (*calmly*). I'd have my freedom.

JIM (*likewise*). Fuck yer freedom. Now, take my boot to the cobbler.

FARADAY *has returned, bringing an elegant Frenchman in fashionable clothes* – LAGARDE – *who approaches* JIM *with a small package*.

LAGARDE. Ah, monsieur.

LAGARDE *presents* JIM *with a small package and begins a private exchange as, behind, an attractive, well-dressed black woman,* MARY CLEERE, *lingers in the doorway.*

SMITH. The Frenchman was called Lagarde, and we shall have more of him anon, but while Mister Trumpett was thus engaged, Mister Blanke's notice had been captured by the woman who trailed behind. For though he could not prove it so, he had an uncanny sensation this lady was, if not a personage familiar to himself, then possessed of a extraordinary resemblance to the same.

JIM. John?

BLANKE (*snapping out of reverie*). Is that all, sir?

JIM (*handing package*). And a pacquet for the post.

BLANKE. To the same address as the others?

JIM. Aye.

BLANKE *starts to exit, passing the* WOMAN.

SMITH. And within closer proximity, he took note of two things: first, that he was ever more certain of her identity –

BLANKE (*to* MARY, *as he passes*). Your servant, ma'am.

MARY *ignores* BLANKE's *gaze.*

SMITH. – and secondly, that she had perfumed herself with an essence of gardenias.

JIM *and* LAGARDE *shake hands.*

Chapter Five.

Music. A banquet table is brought into the same position as the CONGREGANTS' *table in Act One, set with lace tablecloths, candelabra, etc. A title reads 'AUGUST'.*

It was Mrs Low's particular custom to hold her end-of-summer soiree on a Tuesday, being the less-coveted weeknight of the social calendar. The invitations specified music and dancing, to be followed by a light supper and a piece of entertainment. And at half-past six a bell was rung summoning all to table –

A SERVANT *rings a bell.* DELILAH *flits into the room, inspects place cards, switches two of them, tears up one, and skitters out again.*

– where the menu was to be as follows: (*Reading from a card.*) Oyster soup with sherry, asparagus *mayonnaise*, cod cakes or jellied crab, crown roast of mutton, kidney pie with garden peas, and frozen sweet cream with brandied cherries for pudding.

DELILAH *returns, bringing* SHIRLEY *on one arm. In the other she carries a small, gaily painted metal pail with a lid, a slot. As she speaks, she gives it a shake to demonstrate its being filled with coins.*

DELILAH (*to* SHIRLEY). And once we've collected all the shiny coins we join them with those from all the other little pails, and then carry them to the parson who sends them off to the poor little African children!

SHIRLEY. Ah, well done.

DELILAH. It's so tragic, isn't it, to think of them in their dirty little huts?

SHIRLEY. Aren't you industrious.

DELILAH. Mama says I'm her worker bee!

SHIRLEY. Does she?

DELILAH. She calls me Little Lilah Bumble! O, how convenient!
You're seated next to me!!

MARGARITA *bustles in through one door…*

MARGARITA (*to* DELILAH). Darling! What have we asked you?

DELILAH (*defensive*). But I'm taking collection!

MARGARITA (*as she exits, to* JIM). Shall we take our places,
then?

JIM. Thank you, ma'am.

…and out the other, passing JIM, *who hastily ties a cravat as
he enters.* LOW *enters from one direction, while* BLANKE –
in powdered wig and finery – enters from another.

LOW. Are we not seated?

SHIRLEY. I'm seated.

DELILAH. *I'm* seated.

LOW. The bell was rung.

JIM. I *would* be seated, sir, could I find my place card.

DELILAH (*shaking her pail, to* SHIRLEY). I do hope *you'll* be
making a contribution to Africa, Colonel –

SHIRLEY. Mmmyes…

DELILAH (*pointedly, re:* JIM). – unlike *certain* miserly people.

LOW (*re: collection bucket*). Not at the *table*, Lilah.

DELILAH (*petulant*). *Does no one care about the little dusky
babies?*

LOW. But *later.*

DELILAH *exits sulkily with her pail, passing* MARGARITA,
who is escorting MARY.

MARGARITA (*to* MARY). Les étés sont très belles dans le sud
de la France. [The summers are so lovely in Southern France.]

MARY. Oui, madame.

LOW (*to* MARGARITA, *as he exits*). Should we ring again?

LOW *exits past* MARGARITA *and* MARY.

MARGARITA. Et je suis terriblement friands de le fromages doux! [And I'm terribly fond of the soft cheeses!]

JIM. Lady?

MARGARITA. Jim?

JIM. My chair?

MARGARITA. Have you not a place card?

JIM. 'Twould seem to have gone missing.

MARGARITA. O, vexation – (*To* MARY, *re:* BLANKE.) Ah, oui! Ici c'est Monsieur Blanke. Il est très intéressant!

And suddenly BLANKE *is trapped with* MARY.

(*To* JIM.) Let's just have a look, then, shall we?

MARGARITA *inspects place cards, as:*

BLANKE (*overcome with nerves*). I – I – I, erm, do hope you may forgive the effrontery if one was to venture to... address you in the familiar case?

MARY. Pardon, monsieur, je ne compren–

BLANKE. You understand me well enough, do you not? For I seem to think I know you.

MARY (*perfect English, no French accent*). I should think that most unlikely, sir –

BLANKE. Your name is *Mary*, is it not?

MARY *goes still*.

Mary *Cleere*? For in my youth, I did know a girl of such a name.

SERVANT *passes through, ringing the bell again*. DELILAH *has returned to find* JIM *seated*.

DELILAH (*to* MARGARITA). But that place was reserved for Mister *Blanke*!

MARGARITA. Let's not be quarrelsome!

JIM. And I'm sure he'll be happy to accommodate, eh, John?

BLANKE. Hm?

DELILAH (*to* JIM). But we're nearly at capacity!

JIM (*seating himself*). 'Twill be all the merrier, then.

> DELILAH *sits, sighs, in misery.* LOW *returns with other guests, as* MARGARITA *exits, and* –

BLANKE (*quietly, turning back to* MARY). The lady of whom I speak and myself were separated by cruel design, and I did make promise should I ever again hear tell of her, or the surname *Cleere* – for they did leave a clear space where the surname should be upon her christening page –

MARY. Good sir –

BLANKE. 'Tis *John*. As I'm confident you know – (*Continues.*)

MARY (*overlapping*). May I stop you?

BLANKE. – and what I would tell her – were that meeting to occur – is that in all the intervening years – (*Continues.*)

MARY (*quietly overlapping*). This conversation is unwise, and –

BLANKE. – I've never once forgotten the passionate vision we shared of a future that was not to be – nor lost hope it would some day come to pass –

> MARGARITA *re-enters.*

MARGARITA. Who are we missing?

JIM. Mister Lagarde, ma'am.

LOW. – the devil is he?

JIM. Just outside, sir.

MARGARITA. The soup will grow cold!

JIM. I'll just fetch him, then? (*Winking at* DELILAH.) If mam'selle will defend my chair!

LOW (*seating himself*). Good lad!

> JIM *exits.*

DELILAH (*whispered fury*). *Mama!*

MARGARITA. Try to be civil, darling.

DELILAH. But why must he *pester* me so?

MARGARITA. *Shhhhh!*

BLANKE (*to* MARY). My master's master is scrupulous in matters of justice, and were I to put it forth I might well interest him in procuring your release from this strutting woodcock whom you now do serve –

MARY (*gently*). Mister Blanke –

BLANKE. Can you not so much as say my *name*?

MARY (*beat, carefully*). – you did live in conditions of opulence once – John – and 'tis your good fortune to do so once again –

BLANKE. And what of it?

MARY. – then, might one recommend you take stock of what you have?

BLANKE. And what is it worth, finally?

MARY (*sensibly*). Why, rather a great deal, I should think.

   JIM *returns with* LAGARDE.

LOW. Here we are, then! | MARGARITA. O! At last! | JIM. Found him, sir! | LAGARDE (*to all*). Veuillez m'excuser, mes amis!

BLANKE (*to* MARY). She that I knew in childhood would have disdained such complaisancy.

MARY (*beat*). Then I shall wish you success in finding her.

   LOW *taps a knife against a glass. Music stops. All take seats as* LOW *speaks.*

LOW. My friends, before we tuck in, I feel bound to share a piece of news that has only now been divulged to me by my dear Colonel Shirley. Colonel:

SHIRLEY (*standing*). Mmmyes. Well, it pleases me to report that, not three hours prior to this gathering, General Howe has engaged the insurgent forces with overwhelming firepower and driven them into cowardly retreat as far as the Palisades of Brooklyn –

All applaud, some say 'Huzzah!' 'Hear, hear!', etc.

– and with that, may we finally bring an end to these present disturbances.

LOW. And I've asked the Colonel to convey to His Majesty our shame for this gross misbehaviour on the part of our countrymen, of a type thankfully uncharacteristic of these colonies. (*Raising his glass.*) And secondly – yes, Jim?

JIM. Might *I* raise a glass, sir?

LOW. Erm –

JIM. To yourself, that is?

LOW. Ah –

JIM. For, as one who never did know the solace of a father's tender affection, may I here give publick thanks for that benevolent hand that was so warmly extended to me where my own was wanting.

LOW. Not at all –

JIM. And also to *Mrs* Low –

LOW. Ah, yes.

JIM. – who so commands the admiration of her company that they would engrave her name above the door of ev'ry charitable establishment in town.

MARGARITA (*demurely*). Not *ev'ry*.

LOW. Very good. And sec–

JIM. And lastly a *curse*.

LOW. How's that?

JIM. A curse *upon* and a farewell *to* that *fever* that forbade me the pleasure of *Miss* Low's company only last week at Delancey

Square, and from which I trust she's now made complete recovery.

MARGARITA (*quietly to* DELILAH). A *fever*?

DELILAH (*to* JIM). Not completely, no.

LOW. All done, are you?

JIM. All done.

LOW. All done – errrm - what was I – ?

MARGARITA. You'd raised your glass?

LOW. Exactly – may we all raise a glass in anticipation of the evening's *dramatic* offering by Mister John Blanke, the educated Negro, with an aim to enlighten us –

MARGARITA. – *and* uplift!

LOW. – and *in* that spirit I have asked him to dine with us tonight at our table: John.

MARGARITA *whispers to* BLANKE, *who stands awkwardly. Polite applause.*

BLANKE. Ah. Well – I do thank Mister Low for his words, and would only offer my gratitude for this opportunity to speak – albeit in theatrical form – on a matter of some grave concern, not only for myself, but, in a very real sense, for all of man–

LAGARDE (*his hand has been raised*). Mister Blanke?

BLANKE. Sir?

LAGARDE (*with a laugh*). Forgive me – I am not, erm, as you would say, a man of sophisticated tastes, you know? But, your intention, if I understand, yes? Is *political* in nature?

BLANKE. My intention –

MARGARITA (*interceding*). Mister Blanke's presentation, is *autobiographical*, and shall address the larger question of the Negro and his future status, and as one who has seen an earlier incarnation –

SHIRLEY. D'ye know – I once saw a fellow in Buxton who could play the *fiddle* with his *feet*.

LOW. Did you?

DELILAH (*sadly*). Had he no *arms*, then?

SHIRLEY. No no. For comic effect.

MARGARITA. But – but – but *I* feel that a work of *dramatic* intention can prick our hearts by shewing us the *humanity* of those depicted – and – and – and when we *embrace* their sufferings –

LAGARDE. No no, madame. I only meant to ask Mister Blanke – I am curious – Is there, do you think, a *profit* to be made?

BLANKE (*beat, then, with distaste*). *Profit*, sir?

LAGARDE (*to* MARY, *confirming his translation*). 'Profit', oui?

MARY. Profit.

LAGARDE. Profit, yes. Is there a – a – a – *market* for –

BLANKE. For what, exactly?

LAGARDE. Diversions, erm, such as this one of yours?

MARGARITA (*excited*). *Might* there be?

BLANKE. 'Twas never my aim to *divert*, but rather to edify.

MARGARITA (*with a merry laugh*). O! Think of it, Zacky! If John could be *rich*?

BLANKE. Money, ma'am, is gratefully not the sole determinant of a man's actions.

DELILAH. Nor a *lady's*.

JIM *cackles to himself.*

LAGARDE. But – there is no *shame* in gold, is there? How else would you have us conduct the business of living, eh?

DELILAH (*to* BLANKE). And gold *is* the colour of honey, and I *do* love honey so!

MARGARITA (*generally*). O, she does.

DELILAH. Three spoonsful in every cup!

BLANKE. There are few –

JIM (*attempting to flirt*). Do you know what honey *is*, lady?

DELILAH. Nor do I care to.

JIM. 'Tis what the bees regurgitate.

BLANKE (*ignoring* JIM, *to* LAGARDE). There are few things a man does prize more than gold, I grant you, but I do know of one.

LAGARDE. And what is that, monsieur?

MARGARITA. Shall we have a guessing game?

BLANKE. His *freedom*, ma'am – (*Continues*.)

LOW. Well, in *theory*, yes, but as a *practical* matter –	MARGARITA. Oh, yes. Well, certainly. It's *frightfully* important.	BLANKE. – as you'd have surely surmised?
DELILAH. *And* mine! When shall I have freedom? Never!	SHIRLEY. Oh, *that*. Well.	LAGARDE (*to* BLANKE). But that is a matter of great complexity, yes?

LOW. But: *if* tomorrow I was to say to you, John, this house is yours and all it contains? Horses to ride –

LAGARDE. Servants to attend you?

LOW. – *or:* you could have your *freedom* and naught else –

BLANKE. Without hesitation.

LOW. But – but – but – think carefully, John – (*Continues*.)	MARGARITA. O, *John*! It pains me to think of it!	DELILAH. As would I!!

JIM. Make *me* the offer, sir. I shall answer plainly!	SHIRLEY. Is this a foretaste of the performance to come?

LOW. – You would wander the streets, then, a penniless nomad – ?

MARGARITA. *Say not so!*

LOW. – Preferring a life of itinerant hardship?

BLANKE. Did those who first journeyed to this continent, sir, do so for *monetary* advantage – ? (*Continues.*)

| LOW. But the two are inextrica-bly – | MARGARITA. Wasn't it partly for the unspoiled landscape? | BLANKE. – or did they, rather, *risk their lives* – (*Continues.*) |
| JIM. What advantage would ya have? | DELILAH. I've an abhorrence of sea travel! | SHIRLEY. I've a word or two I'd like to say, if I might? |

BLANKE. – in the worthy pursuit of greater *freedom*?

SHIRLEY (*to* BLANKE). My good fellow: the colonies are a primary source of *revenue*.

LOW. And were you to take away the competitive *advantage* we enjoy, by eliminating that labour force you would render them instantly worthless.

SHIRLEY (*to* BLANKE). Why else would we *fight* for them, you silly tit?

LOW. And why else should the colonists resist?

LAGARDE. *Exactement.*

BLANKE. I – I – can we not as easily *employ* labourers at a decent *wage*?

LOW (*gently*). Well – but then there would be no *profit*, John, and industry would collapse. And if you cripple industry, well, you only create general impoverishment. (*Beat.*) Now, *that's* no good, is it?

BLANKE *is appalled, at a loss for an answer.*

(*Careful not to upset him.*) All great economies had slaves, John.

SHIRLEY. Indisputably.

LOW. The Egyptians –

SHIRLEY. The heathen Chinee.

DELILAH. Didn't the Romans, Papa?

LOW. Oh, I should say. The Ottoman Turks –

BLANKE. And would you have us no better? (*Continues.*)

LOW. But – but – aren't we really all the *same*, on some level?	MARGARITA. But we *are* better. We're more *compasssionate*.	BLANKE. Or would you be like one of these tradesmen of a tropical plantation – (*Continues.*)
JIM (*to* LOW). Yet they are *gone*, sir, and we endure.	DELILAH (*to* SHIRLEY). I'm sending a box of my dresses to Africa!	SHIRLEY (*overlapping, to* DELILAH). Are you, now? Bally good.

BLANKE. – who does purchase human lives like so many oxen to replenish those that daily perish by toiling in their sugar fields?

LAGARDE. *I* cultivate sugar cane, Mister Blanke. That is *my* trade.

BLANKE (*simple, ugly*). Then get yourself into the field and harvest it.

Pause. Discomfort.

MARGARITA (*very quietly, to* DELILAH). Could I have the salt cellar?

BLANKE (*fired up, to* LAGARDE). It is presently by Mister Low's *indulgence*, sir, that I do dine at his table, as you indulge *your* serving-lady this night, but in due course, I tell you, it shall be unexceptional – (*Continues.*)

MARGARITA (*overlapping*). John – ?

BLANKE. – else we who do suffer by it, here amongst you, shall rise up and *make* it so.

MARGARITA. John – ?

LOW (*quietly dissuading her*). Pearlie –

MARGARITA. – Miss Cleere, is – is – is… erm, not a *serving-lady*.

LAGARDE (*to* MARY). Que voulait-il dire?

MARY. Que j'étais une femme de chambre.

LAGARDE *and* MARY *laugh. He kisses her hand.* BLANKE *stares.*

BLANKE (*to* MARY). You cannot possibly mean you are *bride* to this fellow?

LAGARDE (*with a Gallic shrug and a wink, to* BLANKE). Ehhh… well, not as such, Mister Blanke, but a man must have his companion, yes?

BLANKE *is appalled.*

And you will not tell my wife, I trust!

MARGARITA (*taking over*). Our dear Mister Blanke, has suffered an *inordinate* amount of tragedy in his life, and as you will observe in his re-enactment –

BLANKE. Nay, madam. Nay. (*Beat.*) I am sorry. Forgive me, but I rather think I shall decline.

LOW. O, *really.* There's simply no need.	MARGARITA. But you're the very reason we're here!	BLANKE. I'm afraid I fail to see the purpose – (*Continues.*)
JIM. Ya'll do as yer commanded.	DELILAH. But I've invited all of my friends!	SHIRLEY. Oh, for heaven's sake, get on with it.

BLANKE. – for why should I divert you with airy notions for which in truth you care not a farthing?

MARGARITA. *Not so!*

LAGARDE. No no, madame. We shall have occasion in years to come.

BLANKE. No, that you shall *not*, sir, let me assure you. Not if I play any part in it.

LAGARDE (*with an apologetic laugh*). But sadly, my friend, you do *not*.

All stare at LAGARDE.

Ah… I have said too much.

MARGARITA. I'm afraid I've rather lost the thread of – (*To* LAGARDE.) – why has he no part?

JIM (*to* BLANKE). Mister Lagarde, John, is to be your new master.

Pause. Then MARGARITA *bursts out laughing.*

MARGARITA. O Jim!! How wicked of you!! You gave me such a frightful – Oh.

But then she realises he is serious.

LOW. Hang on –

DELILAH (*horrified*). *Papa?*

LOW. No no no no no. – He's only having us on, yes, Jim?

JIM. Well… the ink is scarcely dry, sir, I do admit –

MARGARITA (*heartbroken*). *Sold*, you say?

JIM. Of necessity, ma'am –

BLANKE (*re:* LAGARDE). To *this* man?

JIM (*to* BLANKE). And ya always told me, didn't' ya, 'twas yer fondest wish to be free of me? Well, here 'tis granted.

LOW. I – I – I – I – and when was this decided?

JIM. Last week, sir.

Silence. DELILAH *bursts into horrible tears.*

SHIRLEY. Oh dear.

MARGARITA. Well, I – I – I – I suppose it's really not ours to question, but –

DELILAH (*to* JIM). *You're a hateful beast and I shall forever despise you.*

DELILAH *rises, runs from the room, sobbing*.

LAGARDE. Mister Blanke, madame, is an exceptional fellow and we shall be fortunate to call him –

BLANKE. Nay, sir. (*To* JIM.) Forgive me, but I cannot nor will I ever serve this man.

JIM. Well, there's a bill o' sale says otherwise.

BLANKE. Nay. I'll not be another bauble in his repository – (*Re:* MARY.) like *this* trinket that so willingly dangles here upon his arm. For *any* price.

MARY (*privately to* LAGARDE). – ne me sens pas bien. (*Generally.*) Excusez-moi.

MARY *rises, curtseys, exits. More silence*.

MARGARITA. I… feel certain, John, Mister Lagarde would gladly reconsider, knowing how we feel, were we to offer him a competitive –

BLANKE (*blowing up*). *I'd no more be sold to you than he, ma'am!* It matters little to me which one of you does *make purchase* of me, 'tis equally *obscene*.

MARGARITA *covers her mouth, rises, exits. Others follow suit*.

LOW. Well. I believe an apology might be in order.

BLANKE. She need not apologise, sir –

LOW (*exploding*). *Not from her!*

BLANKE. From *whom*?

LOW (*to* BLANKE, *re:* LAGARDE). And secondly to *this* man –

BLANKE. I shall *never*.

LAGARDE (*to* BLANKE). Then, let me to offer *my* apology to *you* –

BLANKE. I'll not accept it.

LOW. *Of all the ridiculous* – (*To* JIM.) Fetch my ledger. (*To* LAGARDE.) Whatever you gave for him, sir, I will double the price. – (*Continues*.)

LOW. – Or	BLANKE.	JIM. I cannot,	LAGARDE.
triple, then.	And do not	sir. 'Tis not	No no no no
(*To* JIM.)	barter with	possible at	no –
And pen	my life, sir,	present.	monsieur,
and ink. We	it discredits		s'il vous
can settle	us both.		plait – I
this at once.			cannot
			accept.

LOW (*exasperated, to* LAGARDE). – or what you'd have for him, then.

LAGARDE. I cannot accept, my friend, because the funds are not yours to dispose of.

LOW (*beat*). Are not – ?

JIM. You recall, you did make promise to compensate Mister Lagarde for his losses. And Mister Blanke is one part of a greater bundle of assets transferred to offset that loss.

Small pause. SMITH *has entered.*

I can well explain –

LOW. Yes, do.

JIM. – but it hardly seems fit topic for the present occasion.

LOW. The ladies are gone.

JIM. But, p'raps at a more agreeable opportunity?

LOW. It agrees with me now.

JIM. Very well. (*Simply, with a shrug.*) There was a shortfall.

SHIRLEY. Oh dear.

LOW (*not panicking yet*). Yes?

JIM. Two or three investments simply failed to return as expected –

SHIRLEY. Oh dear.

LOW. Yes?

JIM. And Mister Lagarde, has generously agreed to accept some of our variable assets in lieu of the – (*Continues.*)

LOW (*overlapping*). Such as?

JIM. – immediate monetary – Sir?

LOW. To which assets do you refer?

JIM. Various – assets, such as my servingman, or this household –
(*Continues.*)

LOW (*overlapping*). *My* household?

JIM. – to be held temporarily, until the monetary settlement was
fulfilled –

LAGARDE (*to* LOW). Was none of this explained?

LOW. And how was it fulfilled?

JIM. Sir?

LOW. The settlement.

JIM. Well. (*Beat.*) 'Twas necessary to liquidate a portion of the
equity fund, *and yet* –

LOW (*still not totally panicked*). What portion?

JIM. – I've prepared to recirculate it in such a way that –

LOW. What portion?

JIM. – that come *third* quarter of next year –

LOW. Jim. I'm asking you to tell me how much has been lost.

JIM. Here and now?

LOW. If you would?

JIM (*beat*). Mister Low –

LOW. There was a substantial *surplus* when we took you on, Jim,
that you did assure me was safely leveraged against a host of
ventures that would return at a modest profit. And I'm asking
you to tell me what portion of that is now *forfeit*.

JIM (*beat*). You did give your signature.

LOW. *God damn you, how much?*

JIM. Some seventy per cent of the principal.

Pause. LOW *takes a deep breath.*

LOW. And how is it to be recovered?

JIM. It – it – it – it cannot be '*recovered*' –

LOW. *Cannot?*

LAGARDE. My friends –

LOW (*finally losing it*). *Seventy per cent?*

JIM. – but I've found a rather ingenious method –

LOW. *Seventy?*

LAGARDE. There is simply no need –

LOW (*to* BLANKE). Had you knowledge of this?

BLANKE. None, sir.

LOW. *What has he done?*

BLANKE. I cannot say.

LOW (*to* JIM). *Seventy?!!!*

JIM. Seventy-five?

BLANKE. I only know that each week I do post a parcel to Massachusetts for this man.

LOW (*beat*). And what are the contents?

BLANKE *hesitates.*

JIM (*re:* BLANKE). *He's a filthy fuckin' liar, sir –* (*Continues.*)

JIM. – *a scur-*	LOW.	SHIRLEY	LAGARDE (*to*
rilous and	*Enough!! I*	(*sternly, to*	LOW). I
well-known	*have asked a*	JIM). Here –	know
enemy of the	*question and*	Let's not	nothing of
truth!!	*I'll have it*	have any	this, my
	answered	smutty talk.	friend you
	straight-		must believe
	away!!!		me.
	(*Continues.*)		

LOW. – Now, tell me. What has he posted to Massachusetts?

BLANKE. To – to – to the best of my knowledge… They are banknotes, sir.

Drum roll. A title reads: 'CROWN POINT, MANHATTAN.' The tables and chairs are repositioned for a trial. JIM *stands before* SHIRLEY *as an* OFFICER *takes up a position by his side.*

SMITH. But as the city was under occupation by the English Army and courts of justice suspended, a military tribunal was hastily convened, with Colonel Shirley acting as magistrate, and witnesses brought to testify, some on Mister Trumpett's behalf, and some against.

OFFICER 2 *marches* MRS TRUMPETT *into the room, her hands manacled before her.*

(*Looking at notes.*) You are the adoptive mother of the prisoner, are you?

MRS TRUMPETT (*weakly, near tears*). Aye, sir.

SHIRLEY. By the like name of Trumpett?

MRS TRUMPETT (*almost inaudible*). Aye.

SHIRLEY. And is it not true that, in attempting to recover the monies he did misappropriate from his employer, that the constable did excavate beneath your establishment and in so doing, uncover the remains of both an English officer and one other in an advanced state of decomposition?

MRS TRUMPETT (*breaking down*). Please, sir – O, please, I beg of ya –

SHIRLEY. Or is that not the case?

MRS TRUMPETT. They had no call to treat us in such a fashion –

SHIRLEY. Yes or no?

MRS TRUMPETT (*beat*). Aye, sir.

OFFICER 3 *marches* TIZZY *into the courtroom, likewise manacled.*

SHIRLEY. And have we not also corroborating testimony from one of your domestics that she herself did witness the taking of these lives at the hand of the accused?

OFFICER 3 *gives a shove to* TIZZY, *who shakes her head, mutters, unintelligibly.*

Louder, please?

OFFICER 1. We do, m'lud.

MRS TRUMPETT (*in tears*). They caned us both 'cross the withers, Jim, with a hickory rod –

SHIRLEY. And did she not further testify that he who took these lives may be identified by a distinctive... erm, *blemish*? Upon his – ?

OFFICER 1. She did, m'lud.

SHIRLEY. And has the officer performed the necessary... confirmation?

OFFICER 1. If m'lud would care to see?

SHIRLEY. No no –

LOW *thrusts a sheaf of pages at an* OFFICER, *who hands them to* COLONEL SHIRLEY.

LOW. I did entrust this fellow with safekeeping of all accounts under my direction – Of which some sixty-five per cent are now irretrievably lost to his confederate –

SHIRLEY. Where is the Frenchman?

OFFICER Under sail for Barbados, m'lud.

LOW. – and while this costly misadventure is disaster enough, there remains an additional forfeiture of twenty-five hundred guineas, still unaccounted for.

SHIRLEY (*to* OFFICER 1). And were none of these recovered?

OFFICER 1. Not as yet.

SHIRLEY (*to* MRS TRUMPETT). And will you now reveal their whereabouts?

MRS TRUMPETT (*breaking down*). Can ya not recall me, sir? I'm she what used ta do ya many a good turn – (*Continues*.)

SHIRLEY (*overlapping*). Yes, yes.

MRS TRUMPETT. – and all I ever asked was that the boy might do better'n *I* done.

LOW (*to* SHIRLEY). 'Tis not only myself bears the loss. (*Reading from a list.*) I have here some seventeen homes in greater New York that are now to be seized, some twenty-two businesses in default and a small armada of trading vessels that must remain anchored without cargo. And when confronted with these facts he did reply that such was the acceptable risk of doing business in a competitive market.

SHIRLEY (*eyeing* JIM). Well, sir. You stand accused of a rather comprehensive wickedness. Before judgment is passed, have you anything to say in your defence?

JIM. I do.

SHIRLEY. Briefly, then.

JIM (*clears his throat*). Firstly, I do reject the legitimacy of this proceeding, as your honour is an intimate of the fella what does here accuse me – (*Continues.*)

SHIRLEY (*overlapping*). The claim is irrelevant.

JIM. – and, if Mister Low would bring complaint against some party, 'tis rather my valet and not I should answer fer the charge.

SHIRLEY. Who is this?

OFFICER 1. The Negro, m'lud.

SHIRLEY. Bring him forth.

OFFICER 1. Erm. Likewise, m'lud –

LOW. The fellow took flight some four days ago and is not to be found.

SHIRLEY (*with a sigh*). O, *balls*.

JIM. A notorious villain, sir. Whose disappearance is proof enough.

SHIRLEY. Yes – Leaving that aside, *you've also slain two men* –

JIM. 'Tis but hearsay.

SHIRLEY (*re:* MRS TRUMPETT *and* TIZZY). – *to which these are sworn witness!*

JIM. And secondly: I'd ask the court take account of the lifelong mistreatment I've suffered at the hand of my father – (*Continues*.)

LOW. 'Tis *yourself* bears this shame, sir. Look no further.

SHIRLEY. No no. We shall permit him his say.

JIM. – the treasonous General Washington, who even now does sit atop his charger, in open defiance of the Crown while his own poor issue – that is, myself, sir – does moulder in a prison cell. And I have sent letters so informing him, to which, once received, you may expect swift reply.

SHIRLEY (*bored*). Have we reply?

OFFICER 1. None, m'lud.

SHIRLEY. Moving on.

OFFICER 1 (*producing a letter*). Yet, I do have a statement from a Dr James Craik, Physician General to the Continental Army and confidant of the man hereby implicated.

SHIRLEY. Read it out.

OFFICER 1. Which does attest that the aforesaid Mister Washington was, in his nineteenth year, visited with an infection of smallpox while upon the island of Barbados, as a result of which he was to be rendered… erm –

SHIRLEY. Rendered – ?

OFFICER 1.…incapacitated.

SHIRLEY. In what regard?

OFFICER 1. Erm – ?

SHIRLEY (*to* LOW). What is he saying?

OFFICER 1. In the… reproductive –

LOW. My wife, Colonel, hails from Virginia, as you know, and is something intimate with the Custis family –

OFFICER 1. – That of *Lady* Washington.

LOW. – with whom the fellow did never conceive child. For 'tis widely rumoured – though not for attribution – that Mister

Washington can scarcely perform the marital task upon his
good lady wife.

JIM (*to* SHIRLEY). Slander, sir! *Let the record show I do refute this malicious slander 'gainst my blood and here provide proof of what I say!!*

SHIRLEY (*to* JIM). That is enough. Your complaint is noted and we'll have no more outbursts of this kind!

OFFICER 1 (*to* SHIRLEY). And therefore likely to withstand any claim of paternity.

MRS TRUMPETT. *But we got a letter! Shew 'im, Jim!* (*To* SHIRLEY.) *Ye can see the plain truth of it, sir, from the signature right there at the closing –* (*Continues.*)

JIM *pulls out the tattered old letter, holds it aloft. An* OFFICER *carries it to* SHIRLEY.

MRS TRUMPETT (*to* SHIRLEY). – Mister G. Washington.

SHIRLEY (*dismissive*). Yes yes.

TIZZY (*croaking*). From Virginia.

SHIRLEY. Is that it, then?

JIM. And lastly:

SHIRLEY (*almost inaudibly*). Bloody hell.

JIM. 'Twas only ever my charter to follow the market, sir, what I've faithfully fulfilled, and when that market does miscarry we do but magnify the fault if we would punish those of us most fit to set it right by freer exercise of his business – (*Continues.*)

JIM. – which only flourishes when untethered from burdensome regulation – (*Continues.*)

LOW (*to* JIM). *You'd seem to have confused business with larceny, sir!*

SHIRLEY (*to* LOW). You've *had* your say, now we shall accord him his.

JIM (*to* SHIRLEY). For… there is an *invisible hand*, sir – (*Continues.*)

SHIRLEY (*overlapping*). Say again?

JIM. – the hand what does direct the great movements of capital, cross mighty seas and continents and back again and which, left to its own perfect devising, might uplift even the lowliest – and 'twas never place of man to enquire too closely into its ways nor meddle with its workings, for they only bring misfortune upon themselves that would presume to outmanoeuvre that Great Superintendent of All Things – (*Continues.*)

JIM. – and	LOW (*to*	SHIRLEY (*to*	MRS TRUM-
there will	SHIRLEY).	LOW). No	PETT (*to*
come a time,	*Do you*	no no no no.	SHIRLEY).
sir, mark it	*mean to*	(*To*	'Tis all true,
well –	*permit this*	OFFICER,	sir. He
(*Continues.*)	*nonsense?*	*re:* LOW)	knows
		Silence him,	whereof he
		will you?	speaks.

JIM. – a glorious time when a better nation shall remove the last fetters that hinder us, and prosperity shall flow freely, unencumbered by the chains of obsolescent principle, where the clever and resourceful man, regardless of his station, shall know that when his fellow lies nearby him in the gutter and reaches out his lazy hand for charity, that we must rightly deny him. For we are all of us happiest when we do exceed others, sir, as any man of honesty must finally admit. And 'tis only the fond and childish dream of equality 'twould make beggars of us all.

Pause. SHIRLEY *seems persuaded, then:*

SHIRLEY. Mmmyes. Well. That's rather a startling load of rubbish, isn't it?

JIM. 'Tis an invisible *h–*

SHIRLEY. No no no no no. You are a thief and a liar and quite possibly a murderer, the punishment for which, according to the Lords Commissioners of the Admiralty, is that you be hanged by the neck until such time as you are dead –

Drum roll. A noose descends in front of JIM. MRS TRUMPETT *covers her mouth, stifling a scream.*

– for which likelihood you'd best prepare yourself as the evidence is taken under review.

SOLDIERS *place the noose around* JIM*'s neck and blindfold him as* SMITH *speaks.*

SMITH. But, whereas a market will behave according to the rational self-interest of a *collection* of individuals, the behaviour of any single man is necessarily unpredictable.

An OFFICER *hands a grubby little scrap of paper to* SHIRLEY, *who opens, inspects it.*

For as he was deliberating, an officer had conveyed to Mister Shirley a message from one particular witness, to the effect that, should he show leniency, she would willingly share with him a portion of the illicit proceeds, concealed in a location known only to her –

MRS TRUMPETT *shares a glance with* SHIRLEY, *who subtly acknowledges her, pockets the note.*

– and, as he was a military man, and habitually underpaid, Mister Shirley naturally had his own interests to consider.

SHIRLEY *stands, raises a hand. Drum roll stops.*

SHIRLEY (*clears his throat*). We find the facts arrayed against you are insufficiently dispositive and fail to determine guilt to the necessary standard of certainty.

LOW (*dumbstruck*)....the necess– ?

SHIRLEY. The prisoner is therefore released –

JIM. *Thank you, sir!!!*

SHIRLEY. – and these proceedings at an end.

Music. The OFFICERS *salute* SHIRLEY, *who sheepishly stands, returns the salute, exits.*

JIM. *Justice knows no greater champion than yerself, sir! Ye're a second Solomon, and I shall declare it to all!*

MRS TRUMPETT. O Heaven be praised!! Didn't I tell ya, Jim? I tol' ya justice would be done.

LOW (*stupefied, to* SHIRLEY). Have you lost all semblance of reason? You cannot possibly – *Mister Shirley!!! It is yourself I am addressing, sir!!*

LOW *follows* SHIRLEY, *exiting.* MRS TRUMPETT *and* TIZZY *are escorted out separately from* JIM. *Doors open and* JIM *steps out among the passing pedestrians.*

SMITH. The chamber doors were thrown wide and Jim Trumpett stepped into the bright sunshine to fill his lungs again with the warm breath of freedom, and yet in the very moment of his greatest philosophical triumph the course of his life was to take one last abrupt and fatal deviation –

Music stops. Silence. JIM *stops in his tracks, confused, turns. A knife handle protrudes from his chest. He looks for help – but he is alone.*

The steel blade had severed his pulmonary artery, an injury which, once sustained, precipitates a instantaneous flooding of the chest cavity, leading to the paradoxical circumstance of drowning in one's own blood.

JIM *coughs up blood, staggers, turns blue.*

And had a surgeon been present his life might have been briefly extended, but as it was, he had only time enough to kneel down in the gutter upon a bed of horse manure, as the commercial life of the city continued on about him. And while 'twas variously rumoured the assailant had been a young woman or else a vagabond slave – or one of any number with justifiable cause – the true culprit was ne'er to be found. Leaving some to remark – those of an ironical cast of mind – that the hand which had slain him, had apparently been an *invisible* one.

JIM *is dead. People step around and over him. A* SMALL
BOY *stops to look at the body, only to be dragged away by his
mother.*

But amid this sad ambiguity, you may well have asked, what
had become of Mister Blanke? And how could Mister
Trumpett's progeny survive him, even as he himself came to
this unwholesome end? And now you may be answered.

Title reads: 'EPILOGUE'. JIM*'s body is removed. Snow falls.*
BLANKE *enters at a distance.*

'Twas early November when Mister Blanke, travelling by foot
and under fugitive cover of darkness, did at last return among
the followers of Brother Pugh, where he had previously found
acceptance and upon whom his master had lain curses that they
might never thrive. But *did* they thrive?

The CONGREGANTS – *including* CONSTANCE *and* POOR
TIM (*with the cage on his head*) *bring in a plain wooden coffin
and place benches as they quietly hum 'We Must Be Meek'.*

Sadly, they did not. For shortly before his arrival they had
received a donation of woollen blankets, which proved to be
contaminated with biting fleas, and a deadly contagion quickly
spread among them.

The BRETHREN *encircle the coffin, humming.*

First to take ill was Brother Pugh. His daughter ran door to
door in town, appealing to charity, of which little was to be
had. And when he expired, she wept hot tears of anger.

CONSTANCE *moves her shawl aside and we can see that she
is very pregnant.*

As for herself, she had in the interval grown heavy with the
fruit of Mister Trumpett's molestation. And whereas today a
fetus engendered through violent assault might be terminated
by means of pneumatic suction, Miss Pugh was forced to
undergo the delivery – with Mister Blanke assisting.

CONSTANCE *suddenly grips her abdomen in pain, and is laid
upon a bench to deliver. We hear the sound of an infant's cries,
as* BLANKE *emerges from her skirts with a swaddled baby.*

Whereafter, in her weakened condition she soon surrendered to the illness that had taken her father. Mister Blanke remained at her side until the last, when, at a quarter past two in the afternoon she lifted her head to pronounce:

CONSTANCE. Mister Blanke, while I no longer wholeheartedly believe there may *be* a Creator, still, *if* there be, I do intend to defy Him in the next life, as He has most surely forsaken us in this one.

SMITH. And with that, she too passed.

Her body – as well as the coffin – are carried out by the BRETHREN, *leaving only* BLANKE, *holding the baby, next to* POOR TIM *on the bench. The cage is removed from* POOR TIM*'s head and he immediately begins to babble. The singing ends.*

POOR TIM (*obliviously*).…and cheeses and munny and cheeses and munny and… (*Etc.*)

SMITH. And as the pathogen spread among the rest they did entreat the local physician for assistance. But while those in town had planned and saved for such exigencies, the brethren had given their monies *away* as a matter of faith, and now as one by one they yielded to illness, it must be said that each privately re-examined this policy. For, in six weeks' time, all but three would perish –

BLANKE *hands the baby to* POOR TIM, *reclines feebly upon the bench.*

– and of those three, even Mister Blanke eventually succumbed. He lay shivering upon a pallet for twenty-three days, dreaming of the warmth of coastal Africa, and the sweet aroma of palm wine as his end grew ever closer. And yet… only moments before its arrival, a most curious event was to transpire.

Suddenly, a blinding light illuminates a corner of the stage and a throbbing electromagnetic buzz is heard. An enormous, glowing, golden beehive-shaped object, equipped with landing gear, descends. POOR TIM *stares up in rapture, claps his hands.* BLANKE *shields his eyes.*

POOR TIM (*gleefully*). *Kitten duh beddy-bye da myooo! Kitten duh beddy-bye da myooo!*

The craft lands and two seven-foot tall ALIENS *in the shape of bees emerge, taking readings with various instruments. They communicate via electronic buzzing noises.* BLANKE *lifts his head.*

BLANKE (*feverish*). Are you angels of the Lord now come for me, then? Or from some worser place? Whatever the destination, I shall follow. I only ask first you might tell me, in your wisdom... what is it shall become of us?

The ALIENS *consult with each other, confused.*

– *Mankind*, that is. What shall be the character of our lives, can you tell us, some two, some three hundred years hence?

POOR TIM. Honda your sense!

The first ALIEN *uses a communicating device.*

ALIEN 1. We are advance sentinels from Colony Seven of the Secondary Quadrant. According to our calculations, your population will rapidly expand some two hundred solar years from now, and the resultant rise in atmospheric temperatures will render this habitat unsuitable to your species, at which point we will assume occupancy.

BLANKE. But – but – but – it cannot be.

ALIEN 2. All simian species indirectly engineer their own extermination.

BLANKE. Not so. I do dispute it.

ALIEN 1. Your competitive instincts are sexually determined and exceed your cooperative instincts by a factor of three point six to one. Your collective decisions are made from self-interest, and your lifespans are of such brief duration that the lessons of each generation are lost upon that which succeeds it.

BLANKE. Nay – I never will believe our destinies are so ordained.

ALIEN 2 (*to* ALIEN 1). Sampling sequence complete.

The ALIENS *begin to return to their hive.*

BLANKE. For surely we can *learn*. I know that we can. Tell us, then, in what manner we might reform our ways to avoid this dreadful fate, and we most certainly will do so.

ALIEN 1. Your vital signs will terminate in twenty-seven seconds. We recommend you spend them in contemplation of simpler questions.

The ALIENS *exit as they came.*

SMITH. And as he watched them ascending heavenward, Mister Blanke's breathing quickened, his heartbeat slowed, and he quietly died, precisely to the second they had predicted.

BLANKE *dies.* POOR TIM *is oblivious. Two* MEN *with rags tied over their noses and mouths enter, lift* BLANKE*'s body and roughly carry it away as the snow continues to fall.*

POOR TIM (*quietly, as he rocks the baby*).....cheeses and munny and cheeses and munny...

SMITH. His body was placed in a communal grave and covered in quicklime and earth, in a location, which in years to come, would be paved over with a layer of asphalt as parking space for a Taco Bell, a Pizza Hut, and a Lady Footlocker. And with that, his name came to its end.

The baby begins to cry. SMITH *makes his way to the door from which he originally entered.*

(*As he dons his greatcoat and hat.*) Mister *Trumpett's* name, by contrast, would live on, and his descendants would be numerous and many would prosper. And the wealth thereby created would be multiplied many-fold and with it factories and skyscrapers would be built and houses purchased and yachts and swimming pools and sports cars and racehorses, and a small fraction – a very *miniscule* fraction – would be disbursed as charity – in fact, one or two of his lineage have even contributed funds to the maintenance of this very theatre. Which should come as little surprise. I mean, you don't suppose these buildings are *free*, do you? Someone has to *pay* for them. And who has that money? Not *artists*, certainly? (*Laughs at the very thought.*) Why, *kings*, have it, as they always have, as well as bankers and businessmen and thieves. For if you look *very* carefully, you're sure to find a thief or two in the family tree of every millionaire.

POOR TIM *rocks the baby and chants to himself.*

POOR TIM…and cheeses and munny and cheeses and munny and cheeses and munny….

SMITH. And now we are concluded.

He exits, leaving POOR TIM *and the baby behind.*

End of play.

Other Titles from Nick Hern Books

Mike Bartlett
BULL

Jez Butterworth
JERUSALEM
JEZ BUTTERWORTH PLAYS: ONE
MOJO
THE NIGHT HERON
PARLOUR SONG
THE RIVER
THE WINTERLING

Alexi Kaye Campbell
APOLOGIA
THE FAITH MACHINE
THE PRIDE

Caryl Churchill
BLUE HEART
CHURCHILL PLAYS: THREE
CHURCHILL PLAYS: FOUR
CHURCHILL: SHORTS
CLOUD NINE
DING DONG THE WICKED
A DREAM PLAY *after* Strindberg
DRUNK ENOUGH TO SAY I LOVE YOU?
FAR AWAY
HOTEL
ICECREAM
LIGHT SHINING IN BUCKINGHAMSHIRE
LOVE AND INFORMATION
MAD FOREST
A NUMBER
SEVEN JEWISH CHILDREN
THE SKRIKER
THIS IS A CHAIR
THYESTES *after* Seneca
TRAPS

Ariel Dorfman
DEATH AND THE MAIDEN
PURGATORIO
READER
THE RESISTANCE TRILOGY
WIDOWS

Arthur Miller
AN ENEMY OF THE PEOPLE *after* Ibsen

Bruce Norris
CLYBOURNE PARK
THE PAIN AND THE ITCH
PURPLE HEART

Lynn Nottage
RUINED

Eugene O'Neill
AH! WILDERNESS
ANNA CHRISTIE & THE EMPEROR JONES
DESIRE UNDER THE ELMS & GREAT GOD BROWN
THE HAIRY APE & ALL GOD'S CHILLUN GOT WINGS
THE ICEMAN COMETH
LONG DAY'S JOURNEY INTO NIGHT
MOURNING BECOMES ELECTRA
A MOON FOR THE MISBEGOTTEN
STRANGE INTERLUDE
A TOUCH OF THE POET

Jack Thorne
2ND MAY 1997
BUNNY
MYDIDAE
STACY & FANNY AND FAGGOT
WHEN YOU CURE ME

Enda Walsh
BEDBOUND & MISTERMAN
DELIRIUM
DISCO PIGS & SUCKING DUBLIN
ENDA WALSH PLAYS: ONE
MISTERMAN
THE NEW ELECTRIC BALLROOM
ONCE
PENELOPE
THE SMALL THINGS
THE WALWORTH FARCE

Tom Wells
JUMPERS FOR GOALPOSTS
THE KITCHEN SINK
ME, AS A PENGUIN

A Nick Hern Book

The Low Road first published in Great Britain as a paperback original in 2013 by Nick Hern Books Limited, The Glasshouse, 49a Goldhawk Road, London W12 8QP, in association with the Royal Court Theatre, London

The Low Road copyright © Bruce Norris 2013

Bruce Norris has asserted his right to be identified as the author of this work

Cover image: © feastcreative.com
Cover design: Ned Hoste, 2H

Typeset by Nick Hern Books, London
Printed in Great Britain by CPI Group (UK) Ltd

A CIP catalogue record for this book is available from the British Library

ISBN 978 1 84842 318 3

www.nickhernbooks.co.uk

facebook.com/nickhernbooks

twitter.com/nickhernbooks